About the Author

After being discharged from the army I was employed in numerous jobs: Meat porter, window cleaner, Blackpool Pleasure Beach, biscuit factory, to name a few. Eventually at the age of 36 I got a job at the magistrate's courts.

Drink blighted my life for a good number of years. In desperation at the age of 38 I managed to stop drinking with the help of Alcoholics Anonymous and a man called Tony. Words cannot express my gratitude.

Eventually I started to write poetry, life-in-rhyme. I enjoy sharing my work as a speaker poet. I could never have dreamed that one day I would become a published author at the age of 76.

I have now been sober for half of my life.

Dedication

I dedicate this book to Tony V., a man who came to see me when I was at my lowest ebb in life. He guided and carried me in my early days of recovery from my alcoholism. He was my sponsor and great friend. Sadly, he passed away in 2006. I still miss him.
Thank you Tony.

James Lettice

LONG JOURNEY TO JIMBOPO

AUSTIN MACAULEY™
PUBLISHERS LTD.

A CIP catalogue record for this title is available from the British Library.

ISBN 9781786931368 (Paperback)
ISBN 9781786931375 (Hardback)
ISBN 9781786931382 (E-Book)
www.austinmacauley.com

First Published (2017)
Austin Macauley Publishers Ltd.™
25 Canada Square
Canary Wharf
London
E14 5LQ

Acknowledgements

All my work has been done by pencil to paper, freehand and I would like to thank Carol Broughton for printing it out and getting the whole thing rolling.

Thanks to my friend Charlie for printing out my poetry.

To Peter Connelly for all the encouragement and belief in me, that I did indeed write poetry.

To Rob Thomas who seconded what Peter was saying and for all the help and support he has been in my recovery from my illness. Both of you I thank, from the bottom of my heart.

To Alan for endorsing my story, thank you.

To my wonderful wife of 53 years, I thank you for putting up with me, constantly with pencil and paper in my hand. I could not have had a better person to share my life with.

I thank all my family, for the love and support throughout their lives: son John, daughters Kerry (nee Spencer) and husband Mike; Debbie (nee) Goodfellow and husband Darren. Thank you all.

To Grandchildren: David, who has now introduced a great grandson into my life – Oliver.

To granddaughters, Megan and Cat. I thank you for the joy and laughter we've shared, singing *Great Balls of Fire*" and "*Blueberry Hill*". I love you all.

To my close friends, Clive, Rodney and Noel, thank you for all your support and to my lifelong friend Moz (Maurice) We have been pals for 66 years, a friendship I value greatly.

To my publishers Austin Macauley for taking on an unknown first time old author, thank you.

LONG JOURNEY
TO JIMPOPO

I was born in Wigan, Lancashire in July 1940, a war baby! I was named James after my dad. I had a sister who was two years older than me and her name was Theresa.

I don't know if my dad ever saw me before he was called up to serve King and country. What I do know is that he went off to fight in North Africa, with the 7th Armoured Division, known as the 'Desert Rats'.

After Dad left for Africa, our mother took us to live in Adlington, which is where her side of the family came from. Dad's side lived in Wigan. There were always lots of kids playing in the streets. The boys played with marbles, which we called 'pops', or at 'British Bulldog' and later we would play at shooting Germans, using sticks as guns whilst the girls played at hopscotch or with a skipping rope and we all had to practise running to the air raid shelter and putting on our gas masks. We looked like something from outer space and we would make funny noises at one another.

I must have been about three years old when I started wetting the bed and crying myself to sleep. I was frightened! It was dark outside and we were alone in the house. Our mother was out, she was out most nights. She was in the pub just down the road. Sometimes I was able to stay awake listening for her to come back. I'd be OK then. Sometimes when she came home I would hear voices downstairs but if she came to peep in at the bedroom I would close my eyes tight until she closed the door again. The next morning we would meet an 'Uncle Eric'. After a while a baby appeared but was kept in the back room, only to disappear again shortly after!

The next thing, our dad came home. He was in his army uniform. He had brought me some wooden camels and some silk pyjamas for Theresa. He was only with us for a few days when he left again. He told me he would be back and sure enough, a few days later he came and took me and Theresa from the house.

I didn't know where my sister went, but I was put into a home with lots of other little kids. I think the home was run by the church! It was here where I again started to cry myself to sleep and to wet the bed. The fact that I was then told how naughty I was did absolutely nothing to improve my situation, probably the opposite.

I don't know how long I was in that home but one day my dad turned up with a little brown suitcase, put my clothes into it and off we went. He took me on a bus to Blackpool. When we arrived I was taken to a house in Cunliffe Road where I was to live with my Uncle Tom, Aunt Sally and cousin Celia.

Tom was very stern and Sally wasn't a nice woman at all. She pretended to be nice when my dad was there but she hid her meanness behind a veil of holiness. She purported to be a devout Catholic!

I must have arrived in Blackpool in a bit of a state because I soon became really poorly with scarlet fever. My cousin Celia thought I was going to die but I don't remember much about it except that I was kept in a darkened room. After I recovered my dad moved me again! This time it was back to where I was born – Wigan. I went to live in his parents' house and for the first time in my short life I felt safe.

My grandma was called Phoebe and she came from County Cork in Ireland. She left Ireland as young lass and went to Liverpool where she worked as a 'domestic'. My granddad, Tommy came from Ayr in Scotland where he worked as a coal-miner. He left Scotland to look for work, first in Newcastle then on to Liverpool where he met and married Phoebe. They had four sons: Tom, Harry, Joe and my dad, Jim.

I was happy living with my grandparents and two uncles. They were good to me and even when I wet the bed nobody shouted at me.

I started school at St. Patrick's (St Pat's). It was an old Victorian school and I didn't like it one bit! We were made to go to church and the priests and teachers frightened me to death.

The house where we lived was at the bottom of Platt Lane, in a row of terrace houses called 'The Garden Row'. They were old 'pit' houses and were built sort of back to front. The back of the houses faced onto Platt Lane and the front of the houses faced these massive gardens – hence the name! You couldn't call them gardens really, just overgrown land about 100 yards long. You could get lost there if you wanted to. Good for hiding, especially from Grandma when she wanted me inside. At the bottom of the garden there was a fence about six foot high and on the other side of the fence there were playing fields which we called 'the wreck'.

What a great place the Garden Row was to live! Everybody knew everybody, it was all very friendly and neighbourly and you would see the women scrubbing their front door step, then rubbing some special stone on to it to make it all clean and bright. They certainly took pride in their door steps. They wore long ankle length skirts, shawls over their shoulders and clogs on their feet.

The men would have on wool trousers held up with a wide leather belt, a shirt with no collar, a waistcoat and clogs on their feet and some would wear a neckerchief round their neck. The men would go to the pub after getting their wages and at night, on their way home, they would sometimes throw some coppers to us kids.

We would shout to them, "Hey mister, 'ave you got any spare coppers?"

What else I liked about our street was that we were all in the same boat, just simple, hardworking folk, with lots of heart. The houses only needed a door latch on the outside and a good lock on the inside which was used at night before going to bed. I could simply walk into any house without knocking. I walked into a house one day and Mrs Liptrot was in a tin bath in front of the fire – she didn't bat an eyelid – she just said, "Hello, Jimmy, love. There's a biscuit in the tin in the kitchen!"

I often called in their house to see if they wanted me to go to the shops for them. The best shop was the 'Maypole' which sold just about everything. I would go the corner shop for cigarettes but would only be allowed 3 'Woodbine' and two 'Pasha'. I think 'Pasha' came from the war so you got what you got!! I would also go to the off-licence every night for two bottles of Guinness for Mrs Gaskell. She was a 'happy go lucky' woman who was always good to me and I would sit talking to her.

My Grandma's house was very simple. There was thick lino laid on top of the flagstones and a square table which was covered with a plastic top. Above the table in the middle of the ceiling was a gas light which was lit by turning a little tap and putting a match under the mantle. It was that which made the light glow. There was a big double bed pushed up against the wall in which Gran and Granddad slept. They also had a rocking chair each which were positioned either side of the cooking range. This range was used for all manner of things and was kept clean by Gran spending hours black-leading it. Its main use was the big coal fire with five bars across the front and that fire made great toast! We used a long toasting fork with the bread stabbed on the prongs of the fork and holding it in front of the hot coals. All the cooking was done on the fire and the cast iron pot that stood above the fire was never empty, Grandma would just keep adding to it: scrag end chops, potatoes, carrots, turnip – just about anything, really!! They called it 'Lob Scouse,' probably from their time in Liverpool.

In front of the fire was a peg rug which we made ourselves. All that was needed was a large piece of sack cloth, some old woollen cloth cut into strips and a sharpened wooden peg. The cloth strips were then pushed through the sacking with the peg and 'job was a good un'.

The back room was just flagstones on the floor. There was a big square sink next to which was a big cast iron boiler, a dolly tub, and a mangle. My grandma had to boil my uncle's clothes 'cause Uncle Harry was a miner and his clothes were always black at the end of his shift. Hanging from the ceiling above the fire was a pulley for drying the washing. Trousers, shirts, socks – everything went up there. When the coalman came he would just walk in through the back door, shout, 'Coal' then put three bags full under the stairs. I don't know if it was cheaper or free because of Uncle Harry but I never saw her pay for the coal. The toilet was outside the back door and in the winter it would freeze up which meant we had to flush it with warm water. To wipe our backside we used old newspaper which was torn into pieces and hung on a nail. There was no light out there and in the winter it would be quite a challenge!

We had to take a bucket upstairs at night then empty it in the morning.

Upstairs there was a big double bed in the middle of the room, curtains at the window and nothing else. My uncles slept at the top of the bed and I slept at the bottom between their feet! In the winter we would put a big duck stone in the oven and when it was time for bed Harry would lift the stone out, using a towel, then Joe would hold his nightshirt out at the front in order to carry the stone and off they would march up the stairs, Harry leading the way with a lit candle. Harry would then pull the bedclothes back and Joe would flick the hot stone hopefully into the middle of the bed! Some performance that! The stone was so hot if your feet touched it in the bed you would get third degree burns!

In the early hours of the morning a chap would come down the street armed with a long bamboo pole which he used to tap on the bedroom window. He tapped until Harry or Joe pulled the curtains back and gave a wave.

He was called the 'knocker up' and my uncles paid him at the end of each week. I suppose he was an important member of the community because he made sure the men got up in time to go to work.

Harry was a coal miner, tough as old grout. The pit where he worked was about five miles from home. I would go to meet him sometimes just to walk home with him. A ten mile walk on top of a hard day's labour, but he would always raise a smile when he saw me and he would be as black as the ace of spades except for the whites of his eyes and the white of his teeth. Hanging from his thick leather belt would be two tins: one a drink canister for his tea the other for food which we called 'jack-bit'. Wiganers are known as 'pie-eaters'. This stems back to when the miners ate their pies down the pit. When Harry got home he always had to jump into the tin bath which was in front of the fire and Grandma would be busy boiling the water for it!

Uncle harry had an accident down the pit and the middle finger on his right hand was a real mess. He had a couple of operations to mend his finger and was off work for quite a while. He was sent to recuperate in the Miners'

Home on the promenade near Bispham in Blackpool. When he came home he got upset because the last operation hadn't been a success, his finger was bent over like a hook.

He decided to fix it himself!! He placed his finger over the edge of the table; he then gave me the rolling pin and told me to hit it as hard as I could. Joe was soft hearted so he looked away, as did Grandma. I was only a kid but Harry was pleading with me – so I nodded! He put a towel in his mouth and closed his eyes. I took a deep breath, then 'WHACK'. Uncle Harry was sobbing with the pain and I cried. A few minutes passed and then the colour started to come back into his face. He nodded his approval, ruffled my hair and then off he went with Joe to the infirmary. He could never straighten his finger perfectly but it was good enough for him to be able to go back to work.

Joe had to walk just a couple of miles to where he worked in a forge. This, too, was a dirty job but Joe didn't have a bath when he came home, just a strip wash in the back room.

Wigan was a brilliant place, full of cotton mills, canals, barges, coal pits, slag heaps, a clay pit, a rubber dump, the 'plantations' and of course 'Uncle Joe's mint balls!' What more could a kid ask for! It was wonderful. As soon as I arrived in Wigan from Blackpool my Grandma got to grips with me. She took one look at me, shook her head and gave me a bath in front of the warm fire. When she was drying me she said, 'Just look at thee, lad! Thou's as skinny as a rake 'bout teeth,' and set about building me up. She made steak and cow heel pie and told me it would stick to my ribs. We would eat ham shank with peas, boiled black-puddings, tripe, fish 'n' chips, rabbit pie and I loved her meat and potato pie.

I can't remember ever being hungry when I was there. When I 'played out' I would have either a jam or a treacle butty or sometimes some bread and dripping. It all seemed to me to be such great food but there was a price to pay! Grandma would bring out the castor oil or the malt and cod liver oil and after I had taken this 'medicine' Grandma would say, 'There's a good lad, Jimmy.' She made sure I had food in my belly, clothes on my back and a good pair of clogs on my feet and I grew to love her with all my heart. The clogs had a wooden sole with clog irons underneath. When the irons wore out I would take them to the cobblers and sit in a chair while he put new irons on them. It was a bit like a blacksmith re-shoeing a horse.

We were the only Catholic family in Garden Row, although at the time I wasn't sure of what that meant. Whenever I got into a fight with one of the other kids it was usually just a fall out over something daft and I always stood my ground. We were all pals again in no time but I do remember having a scrap with a lad called Albert. His dad had been stood by his front door watching and he shouted out, 'Go on, son, give him one from me.' I had no idea it was a sectarian thing: come to think of it, most of the other dads were the same! They must have been disappointed as I didn't lose very often. My granddad would stand at the door sometimes and when I came in with a bloody nose he would nod at me and tell Grandma to clean me up. The men eventually took to me and would speak when I passed them in the street. All the women were good to me 'cause I was willing to run errands for them. If I was passing when one of them was baking I would walk in saying, 'By gum, Mrs Blackledge, them cakes smell grand,' reaching out for one as they came out of the oven. I'd get a smack on the back of my hand as she said, 'Now then, Jimmy, let them cool off a bit,' and I would say, 'Do you want anything from the shops, Mrs Blackledge?' 'No,' she would say and then laugh. 'I can read you like a book, you're just the same every time I'm baking. Go on, Jimmy love, you can have one now!'

I was always able to earn money too. Besides doing the errands I used to collect the pig swill on a Saturday with the farmer down the lane, or I'd sometimes go round with the milk cart. I was then able to go to the pictures. It was sixpence at the Hippodrome and fourpence to get in at the 'Labour' which was built above the Wigan Labour Club. The ice cream was served behind the screen! I kissed my first girlfriend in the pictures. She was called Susan Gaskell, we sank down in our seats to be hidden and kissed! I was about eight or nine at the time! The first film to make an impression on me was *The Jolson Story* it was magic and I walked home singing *Mammy*! I've enjoyed singing ever since.

Summers were great. The school holidays seemed long and hot and there were always lots of adventures to be had. The 'rubber dump' was one such place! Tons of tyres left over from the war were just simply dumped, as were large petrol tanks, bullets, empty cartridges plus lots of other exciting stuff. One day I pushed a large tin container into a pond, got a long pole and set off for 'Treasure Island'. Needless to say I didn't get very far as there was a large hole in the container and as I couldn't swim, I finished up very nearly drowning! I stripped off to try to dry my clothes but I still looked a tittle damp when I got home.

My granddad took one look at me and then stood up but he wasn't quick enough because I knew what was coming! I dived under the table, then under the bed. He was trying to hook me out with his walking stick and Grandma was shouting at him to leave me alone. She always tried to protect me. I stayed where I was until he cooled off. Under the bed was my safe place and I needed it!

We used to go to the plantations to play at 'Tarzan'. There was a huge tree with a rope over one of the branches and we took it in turns swinging over what we called, 'The yellow brook'. I did my ape call, beat my chest but sadly, didn't make it across the brook! By the time I got out of the ditch I was covered in yellow slimy clay and my pals were laughing their heads off. They walked in front of me, pretending they weren't with me until we reached Haigh hall. There was a large fish pond there and I got into it to try to clean myself up but when I got home I was back under the bed! It's dead hard trying to take your clothes off whilst trapped under a bed and it took me a long time before I came out from under it that day!

I was always up to some kind of mischief although I didn't like doing anything bad: well, not intentionally, anyway! All of us kids were able to make whatever it was that we needed from what was dumped. We made a trolley cart using two big pram wheels at the back, two smaller wheels at the front, a wooden box to sit in, a bit of rope tied to the front which, along with our feet, we used for steering and away we went, careering down the steep hill – great fun.

I made a catapult to fire at some tin cans but one day I fired it at a bird flying overhead. Never in a million years did I expect to hit it! I got such a shock when this tiny sparrow fell from the sky, still warm and soft. I felt bad and was upset at what I had done. A lesson learned!

Another thing that upset me was when I was on my way home from school one day. I just picked up a bone I saw in the street and threw it at a lamp post. Missed the lamp post, but the bone went *smash,* right through a window in the house where the priest lived. I ran like mad but I wasn't fast enough and when father Kelly turned up at our house I swore blind that it wasn't me. I was stubborn and wouldn't own up. I just kept telling lie after lie. I knew it was wrong but I just stuck to my lies even when Father Kelly told me I would go to hell for blasphemy! Grandma was so disappointed with me. I was eventually expelled from St. Pat's and was sent to St Mary's. I never liked or trusted any of the priests or nuns after that, even though I had caused all the trouble! My grandma had brought me up knowing right from wrong and each time I did something bad, it did make me feel bad. It wasn't that I didn't believe in God, it was just that

I couldn't go to confession anymore as I had 'fallen out' with the priests. I started to pinch stuff and to tell more lies. It was bothering me and I started to dislike myself.

On a Sunday morning when I should have been at church, I was at the back of the houses watching the men gambling and playing 'pitch an' toss'. I soon learnt how to play and it was here that I had my first taste of gambling.

Life in those days was never dull. One day some women were banging on all the doors and more and more women seemed to join them as they made their way down the houses to the end of the lane. They then rolled their sleeves up and set off over the fields. Apparently some chap had done something bad to a little girl and these women were after his blood. A policeman followed the 'pack' but stayed about fifty yards behind! They spotted the man. He was over by the slag heaps. The chase was on! They trapped him like a pack of wolves and then set about him. After a few minutes the policeman stepped forward to take him away and lock him up, saying, 'Now then, ladies, that's enough of that'. What a mess the bloke was in, blood everywhere.

It was over the fields where the canal was. I had some great times on that canal helping the bargemen open the lock gates, jumping on the barge then going down the canal a couple of locks: and it was great fun trying to balance on the lock gates, crossing over them just to fish on the other side of the canal. Every now and then a stretch of the canal would be drained off so it could be cleaned. I was always shocked as to how many dead cats and dogs were in there! How cruel was that? To tie a brick round the neck of the animal and then throw it in to drown! I'd say to myself that it was a good job they didn't do that with people!

When old Mr Gaskell from Garden Row died my grandma said I should go and pay my respects. His body was laid out in the coffin and he had a penny piece over each of his eyes. He was dressed in his best suit and in a shirt and tie. I had never seen him look so smart. I bowed my head and said a little prayer. I hoped he went to heaven!

A short time after that I was to face the saddest time of my life.

I got up one morning and my grandma wasn't there!

Harry and Joe hadn't gone to work.

I knew something terrible had happened.

My uncle Harry sat me down and told me that Grandma was very poorly and that she was in hospital. I went to church and said I was sorry for all the bad things that I had done. I prayed that Grandma would get better. When I went to bed that night I prayed that I would die before her – I didn't think I could survive without her.

The next morning I was told that my grandma Phoebe had died. It broke my heart.

I was ten years old and I started to doubt that there was a god. What would happen to me now?

I later wrote a poem of my time in Wigan, which I dedicated to my grandmother. She was my inspiration and mentor in life, she taught me right from wrong.

My dad, who still lived in Blackpool, came over to see me and told me that I would have to go back to live with Tom and Sally in Blackpool. They had moved to Hornby Road, into a big boarding house with lots of rooms. A few days later my dad came to pick me up. He had a woman with him and he told me that they were going to get married. Her name was Phyllis and she was a waitress in one of the big hotels in Blackpool. I was worried and unhappy about going back to live with Tom and Sally and my fears were proved right.

In the house next door to ours in Hornby Road lived a relative of sorts, I think it was Sally's cousin, her name was Veronica. I was sleeping in the same room as my cousin Celia, who was fourteen years old at that time and she used to tell me things about her mum and dad. I found out that she had an older sister called Margaret but that she didn't know where she was and it took me a long time before I found out.

Tom and Sally hadn't changed one bit. Tom was still very strict and sullen and Sally was still as cruel. What sticks in my mind about her was when we were sat at the table once, eating dinner. We were having stew and there was a big piece of gristle in mine so I took it out of my mouth and put it on the side of my plate. Sally flew round the table, grabbled the gristle and shoved it back in my mouth! I was baulking but she said I couldn't leave the table until I swallowed it. I sat there for about three hours and was eventually sent off to bed with it still in my mouth. I woke up the next day with Sally stood over me and the gristle in her hand! She was a horrid person.

After a short while Dad and Phyllis got married and they got a brand new council house on Mereside Estate.

It had three bedrooms and so Theresa, me, Dad and step-mum became a family.

The school Theresa and I went to was called St John Vianney. Theresa had been living in Blackpool all the time and was already a pupil at that school and so when I went she thought she would look after me, but I could stick up for myself.

I didn't like bullies! Our family name is 'Lettice' which is pronounced Letteese. I had got used to being called Jimmy Lettice in Wigan. No big deal but in Blackpool my sister wanted her name said properly and I agreed. The teachers however thought it very clever to call me 'cabbage,' 'Brussels sprout' or 'summer greens!' Very funny! But whenever a kid called me by any of those names it was a fight – they eventually said our name right! The teachers, however, didn't as they thought it all very funny. Me and my sister looked out for one another and I also looked out for a kid called Tony. Poor lad was paralysed down his left side and he stuttered. When he was picked on I got upset and told them to pick on somebody who could fight back.

School, I suppose was OK but I didn't try very hard at my lessons. When I had an interest in a subject, such as geography, history and even English, I would do well. I was useless at maths and science so I didn't really try. I always wanted to make people like me and I think that was why I was always a bit of a joker.

On the estate where I lived I made a few pals: one of them was called Maurice Berg. The first time we met he was in the process of thumping his kid brother. I told him to pick on somebody who could fight back – he turned round and thumped me on the nose! Of course a fight followed but then somehow a great friendship developed and he was my pal, 'Moz'. There was also Bobby, Billy, Spud, Ray, Billy Forsyth, and Mick Molloy. That was our gang. We knocked around together for a long while and we got up to all kinds of mischief. When we wanted to see a film but only had enough money between us to pay for two, the rest of the gang would wait at the side of the picture house by the fire doors. The two inside would open the fire doors and the rest of us would sneak in and watch the film in guilty pleasure.

I loved playing football or cricket, or any sport, really, although I was never very gifted at any of them and when a team was being picked I was always the fifth or sixth kid to be chosen. Still I always enjoyed it. The summer holidays were brilliant with lots of bike rides, fishing in ponds and giggling as we spied on the courting couples out in the fields. As we got older we would go off to Stanley Park on a Sunday to play at the mini golf or putting, and it was always for two bob each for the winner. It was then onto the lake for a ride in a motor boat with the aim of trying to catch the eye of a pretty girl. I never seemed to have much luck in that department! Life was never boring but quite the opposite, in fact life was great.

I always pretended that nothing scared me and I would do anything for a dare. There was a cemetery not far from where we lived and once in the middle of winter on a dark and stormy night, my pals and I were on our way home when they dared me to walk through the graveyard from one end to the other. 'No problem,' said I! So in I go and they all ran around to the other side. Now I set off nice and slow but with an occasional glance over my shoulder, then I started whistling to myself, more glances over my shoulder and a faster pace, and eventually breaking out into a run, only to slow down again when I could hear my pals making spooky noises. I had frightened myself to death but I certainly wouldn't have let them know it.

Life at home was good too. Phyllis, my step-mum, took good care of me and I suppose she cared for me as she would her own child. The trouble was she treated me as a little boy and she didn't want me to grow up. I was dressed in short pants until I was nearly thirteen – just imagine! When I did eventually get long trousers she said that I looked like a little old man. Phyllis had plans for me. She wanted me to play the piano and very generously paid for me to have piano lessons at the cost of half a crown a session. Like everything else, it didn't come easily to me and after only two lessons I didn't go there again. I did, though, pretend to go but went along to the pictures instead. That was great until after a couple of months of only playing the same couple of notes, Phyllis went off to see the piano teacher! Surprise surprise! no more pictures for me.

My dad just used to shake his head and mutter to himself 'if ever a man suffered!' As I was growing older he said that quite often, because I just kept getting into lots of bits of trouble. It was nothing criminal, just trouble and then when he shouted at me I would tell him stupid lies. Lying was always something that I disliked about myself. I came home from school one day after having the cane from the headmaster I didn't want my dad to find out and I tried to keep quiet about it.

What had happened was that on Thursday mornings before lessons we had to attend mass. The church was built into the school. This particular Thursday at a very solemn part of the service, when the priest was praying, I was telling the lad next to me a joke and we were both trying desperately hard to stifle our laughter. Then the lad could control himself no more and he burst out laughing and so did I! The priest stopped the mass, came down to us and told us to leave the church. I never realized that our headmaster had bright red eyes until I passed him on our way out! When the service finished it was retribution time.

The full school assembled in the hall. The headmaster was standing on the stage, flashing his cane and making it 'swish' through the air. We were walked the full length of the hall and passed my pals, some of whom were pulling faces at us trying to make us laugh and get us into even more trouble. They needn't have bothered, we were already in deep trouble! We went onto the stage, where I was told to bend over. I got twelve lashes. I was glad I had to go first because my friend was a nervous wreck by the time it was his turn. I was always getting punishment of some sort because I was always messing about and I never gave any thought to my future.

I was thirteen with not a care in the world and spent my teenage years with my mates having a laugh and generally just messing around. Saturdays it was going to see Blackpool football team and what a treat it was to watch Stanley Mathews play. Another Blackpool player was called Morty, he played centre forward, and his sister lived down our street. When Blackpool won the cup in 1953 we were all crammed into her house because they were the only ones with a television set. What a day that was! It was just brilliant.

Not many people had a television set but most had a radio and there were some great singers about in those days, Francis Lane and Johnnie Ray being the best two. I knew most of their songs and I still enjoy singing in the bath. (That's not a song, by the way.) 1953 was also the year of the Queen's coronation and so it was back once more to Morty's sister's house to watch it on their television set and the house again was jam packed with friends and neighbours.

I can't remember ever getting pocket money but I did get money for doing a paper round. I had to get up early in the mornings to do the round before I went to school and then did the evening papers after school but before tea. I had to give half my wages to Phyllis but I got it back during the week, by using the money she gave me for school dinners by just having chips from the chip shop. I also had enough money to buy fags because it was around that time that I had started to smoke. During the school holidays I got a job on the 'moss', working in the greenhouses picking tomatoes, lettuce and flowers. I got a shilling an hour, good money!

On a Saturday morning I would walk from the estate to the central railway station pushing a hand cart. I would walk up to four or five newly arrived girls saying, 'Carry your bags, miss?' and then push the cart with their luggage and bags on board to wherever they were staying. We called this 'bagging'! If there were four of them it was two shillings, or for five half a crown. As we walked along the girls always used to sing and they always teased me.

Blackpool seemed just the best place on earth to live. I went out 'bagging' one Saturday morning and earned twelve pounds! I went home and gave my dad five pounds and I remember him fighting back the tears. He only earned about ten pounds a week and it made me feel good giving him that money. I suppose I liked who I was at that time. I always got a good feeling when I tried to help people, especially the old ladies. When I saw one pushing a lawn mower and trying to cut the grass it just seemed a natural thing to say, 'Here you are, missus, I'll do that.' When she went into her purse to give me a shilling, I didn't particularly want it but I knew she wouldn't let me do it again if I didn't take it. If I saw an old lady trying to cross the road I would go and help her, even if I was with my pals. They got used to it and say, 'Eh up, here he goes again!'

The gang of us was getting older and trying to grow up and what a time it was to grow up.

Three films came out in 1954-55 that were to be a great influence on my life. *On the Waterfront* starred Marlon Brando and was about a man who showed great courage in standing up to a mob in a corrupt dockland. Next was *From here to Eternity* with Montgomery Clift. This was about an army private who stood up to everything that was thrown at him, abuse and bullying as well as a lot of other crap. On reflection I think this film probably had a deep and abiding effect on my later life. Then there was rock and roll and *The Blackboard Jungle* with Glen

Ford. He played a school teacher in a very rebellious school. It wasn't the story but the music at the start of the film that was exciting: *Rock Around the Clock*. I had never heard anything like it before and it was like, 'Wow'. Rock and roll had been born and it was also the birth of the 'teddy boy'. I believe the 1950s were the best years ever and mainly because there was lots of work to be had. You could start a job in the morning and if you didn't like it you could start another in the afternoon! Everybody seemed to know each other as you either walked to work or got on the bus. People just seemed to talk to one another.

My sister was now sixteen, nearly seventeen and definitely a rebel. She had changed her name to Terrie and she was staying out till all hours of the early morning so there were lots of slanging matches in the house. It all reached a climax when Phyllis went crazy with her and slapped our kid across the face. She got the shock of her life when Terrie slapped her back. That was it! Our kid packed a bag, gave me a hug then left.

Dad of course was upset when he came home from work to find his daughter gone and it was from then that things began to change in the house. I tried my best to get on with Phyllis for Dad's sake but I began to resent the way she treated him. In the mornings he would walk to his work which was in St. Anne's. This was about four miles away; then on a Friday he would give his pay packet, unopened, to Phyllis. He would then wait to be given his 'spends' but if for any reason he had opened it a shouting match would follow, with Phyllis doing most of the shouting and I would be thinking, 'Don't let her treat you like that'.

I had left school by this time and gone to work as an apprentice upholsterer. I left there after twelve months and got a job in a butcher's shop, where I was able to meet more people and get a better wage. I also enjoyed the patter the butcher gave the women, plus the tips they gave me when I did the deliveries on the shop bicycle.

Following on from *Rock Around the Clock* with Bill Hayley and his Comets came some wonderful rock 'n' roll performers: Elvis, Jerry Lee Lewis, Chuck Berry, Fats Domino and Buddy Holly; they were all absolute icons. My first attempt at being a teddy boy was a failure! I got a Tony Curtis haircut with a 'D.A' at the back! A 'D.A' being a duck's arse! When I got home my dad went berserk. He grabbed hold of me and sat me down in a chair, he then got a bowl out of the cupboard, placed it on my head and proceeded to cut round it! Use your imagination! That was the only time my dad really lost his temper with me. My hair slowly grew again and I also grew some sideburns and eventually got another fashionable D.A!

Getting my first made to measure teddy boy suit was just brilliant. Two of my pals: Moz and Billy Fosythe, who by this time was known as Foz; and Billy Forsythe both conveniently worked in high street tailors' shops. We would swagger about in small gangs, trying to impress the girls. We would get into the occasional fight at the weekend but then it was back to work on the Monday morning.

We spent our time after work playing the juke boxes in coffee bars or just messing about having a laugh. Sunday night was a night that we always looked forward to because we found out about a place in Accrington called 'Joe Mort's' where they had a dance floor and played all the rock 'n' roll records, wonderful! Spud had by this time got a car, a little two seater red sports M.G. which, when he put the hood down, would fit the three of us, sat not on the seats, but on the back of the actual body. Jo Mort's was upstairs in a building on the main road and the first time we went we could hear the music blasting out down the road. It was half a crown to get in. There was no door, just a thick curtain over the doorway. Inside it was so dark you couldn't see a thing until your eyes got used to the dimness.

What a place that was. It was so dark once you were behind the curtain that you just took your chance with who you danced with usually asking the first girl you came in contact with which sometimes proved a bit dodgy, especially if Conway Twitty was singing *Only Make Believe*, a slow ballad! I could be smooching with some gorgeous girl or one who was a bit rough! If it was the latter I made an excuse then disappeared to the pub next door, having got my hand stamped so I could always get back in after a short break! Teds (teddy boys) from Burnley, Blackburn and Nelson and many other towns went to Jo Mort's. We would meet in a pub called

The Crown and when we walked in the cry would go up: "Hey up, here's the Blackpool crowd." We loved it!

It was 1958. I was about 17 years of age and the world was my oyster. Jerry Lee Lewis was coming over from the States to Britain and we got tickets to see him perform in Preston: marvellous. I was going round singing *Great Balls of Fire* all the time and I couldn't wait to see him. Five of us went off to Preston, only to find out he had been kicked out of the country for marrying his thirteen-year-old second cousin. I was absolutely distraught.

National Service was still happening and I believed that some of our gang would be called up, so while we were in Preston three of us joined the army. What a mistake that was! I signed on for nine years and in the July of 1958 I went into the Royal Engineers. I left home with a real bad attitude. Phyllis had told me that she was expecting a baby and that I would need to leave and I vowed that I wouldn't let anyone speak to me how she had spoken to my dad.

On going through the camp gate a song was blaring out, *Who's Sorry Now*! Rather fitting as it happened. I was about to embark on my brilliant military career. On the first morning parade a sergeant called out our names and when he got to mine he shouted, "Lettuce". I stood still; he glanced at me then shouted louder, "Lettuce". Again I stood perfectly still, at which point he stepped forward, looked straight into my face and said, "You're Lettuce, aren't you?" I came to attention and said, "No, Sarge, I'm Lettice". "Oh we've got a right one here," said he. My life was about to take a turn for the worse! I continued to refuse to answer to 'Lettuce' and so my NCOs made my training difficult. Consequently, within a week I was on 'jankers' in the cook house, which was washing pans and peeling potatoes. I wasn't getting back to my billet till late at night and then having to start on buffing my boots and preparing the rest of my kit. I was on fourteen days of jankers and the NCOs were trying to break my spirit. No chance! I could take anything they dished out.

Some of the lads in my billet started to help me out with my kit but that got me into more trouble and I was ordered to parade behind the guard in F.S.M.O., but I had no idea what that was! I found out it was Full Soldiers' Marching Orders'. In other words it meant I had to wear everything I had been issued with. I could hardly stand up straight. An R.M.P. stood at the back of me and when I swayed forward then backwards, he kicked my ankles and told me to stand straight. I turned round and kicked him back! Next thing I'm locked up in the Guard Room and the following morning I'm standing in front of the major! "I've heard about you, LETTICE, and I can't make my mind up if you are a follower or a leader." He said he would be keeping his eye on me and promptly gave me seven more days' jankers.

Basic training only lasted six weeks and I passed out without any further incident. On passing my training, my sister Terrie came to see the parade. It was the first time we had met since she had left home all those years before and it was good to see her looking so well. When some of the lads told her about me she looked surprised and asked me if I was alright. I smiled, gave her a hug and said, "Of course I am, our kid, don't worry about me." It would be four years before we were to meet again.

I was posted to Chatham for 'trade training'. I was going to be a carpenter and joiner! I liked Chatham and made some good mates there. There was Bob from Birmingham and what an accent he had! I went to his house with him on a weekend pass. He stayed just at the back of Winson Green Prison. When we met up with his pals I was in stitches listening to them and I used to tell them that I was the only one who spoke 'proper good English'. We had great times there.

My other pals included lads called Cornish, Jock, Taffy; a scouser called Billy and a lad called Gordon who came from Rhodesia, now Zimbabwe. I think out of all of us Gordon was the one destined to do well in the army because he just got on with things. He was always dead smart and was in his element with regards the discipline, plus he was a good boxer and boxed for the squadron. Gordon thought I was a bit of a nut case but we became good pals and covered each other's backs.

During my training to become a joiner the benches that we worked at were placed back to back and as I turned round, I bumped into the guy at the back of me. He said, "Watch it" and I told him, "Sorry, mate," but he went on to call me a prick and so I told him to fuck off, which is when he came at me with a chisel in his hand! So I let him have it with a wooden mallet! When we went before the major he was the first to speak, he told blatant lies! saying I had been having a go with him for days and yes, he had stood up for himself. When I came to speak the major just didn't listen to me and I never really knew why! Perhaps it was over the bits of trouble I had been in previously.

It was also in Chatham that I began to understand why some squaddies got promoted to lance corporal then corporal: they were 'yes' men, creeps or big mouthed bullies and when a lad couldn't stand up for himself his life was made hell. There was one lad who I wasn't keen on, mainly because he was dirty and smelly and I thought him just a bit slow! Anyway, one day I was on my way to get a shower but the doors to the latrines were shut. I could see through the glass though at what was going on. There were about five N.C.Os. throwing buckets of cold water over this lad who had been stripped naked. They began to scrub him with hard brushes and the lad yelled out in pain.

What made me feel quite disgusted was the look of satisfaction on their faces. I started to bang on the door but when the corporal came to the door he just told me to fuck off. I told him, "You fuck off" and then he threatened me with a bit of the same. I told him if so it would be the last thing he would ever do and hey presto, it suddenly stopped! The poor lad was in a quite a mess. He was scratched and bleeding and curled up in a ball, crying. I asked him which room he was in and went to get him some towels. When he eventually stopped crying and got to his feet I told him, "Look, mate, you brought this on yourself. You can't go round dirty and smelly, this is the army! But what those bastards did to you was out of order and if you want to report them I will go as a witness." He didn't want that, saying he was too frightened and that complaining would only make matters worse. He was probably right! I suppose the N.C.Os. were all waiting to see which way I was going with it. I didn't do anything. But it did open my eyes as to how and why some of those bastards got promoted. There were eight beds to a room in the barracks and all of the lads were OK except for one who was a loner and seemed to act a bit weird. He would come back to his locker late at night and put stuff in it from under his coat. He was strange! The stuff turned out to be ladies' panties and bras which he was nicking off clothes lines. The army soon got rid of him. I got up one morning and was shocked to hear the news that Buddy Holly had been killed in a plane crash. I was gutted. I knew most of his songs by heart and I loved singing them, it was a great loss.

After passing my training at Chatham my posting came through: Singapore! How great was that, I thought? It was a place one could only dream about. I boarded a troop ship in Southampton, it was called the *Nevasa*, and there were about three thousand of us, all going to different parts of the world. We set sail, leaving behind the green pastures of England, on down the Bay of Biscay which was a rough passage. There weren't many of us left on deck for those first couple of days but there was a lot of sea-sickness! I was one of the lucky ones that weren't affected and I loved that voyage. I had only seen things like this in films. As we sailed on towards Gibraltar I thought it was spectacular with Spain on one side, the Rock of Gibraltar on the other and about to enter the Mediterranean Sea. Dolphins joined us and swam in formation at the front of the ship: marvellous.

We docked at 'Gib' as some of the squaddies had been posted there and I enjoyed myself by going to see the Barbary apes and sightseeing round the town. I thought it was a fantastic posting for the ones who were staying but once back on the ship I was looking forward to the next destination.

We set sail for Port Said and the Mediterranean here was a deep blue/green colour, very different from the black waters of the Atlantic and we could see the African continent on our right. As we sailed into Port Said we were met by a barrage of 'bum boats', these were little boats sailed by Egyptians trying to sell us all kinds of things. It was a good laugh bartering! I think they came out on top though. We then sailed through the Suez Canal and it felt very strange, being on a ship yet all we could see was sand. Passed Aden and on through the Red Sea and then entering into the Indian Ocean. I never thought that we could sail for so many days and not see another vessel! It was then that it actually entered my head as to just how vast the ocean was.

Four weeks after leaving the green pastures of England we sailed into the fantastic island of Ceylon, now called Sri Lanka. On entering the port of Colombo we could see a turtle swimming in the beautiful deep green waters. It was massive and I was fascinated.

Colombo was very busy and everybody was trying to get us into their shops to buy or into 'trishaw' to take us wherever: clubs, bars, brothels or to a 'naughty' show! I wasn't ready for the brothels yet so a few of us decided on a naughty show. I didn't want to say anything in front of the other lads but I thought it was 'a bit yuk'; still, it takes all sorts! I had a few beers but I didn't get drunk, I didn't want to chance causing a rainbow over my bed!! Ceylon was amazing, we stayed overnight in the port then set sail the following morning.

We were now on the final leg of our voyage. Singapore, the other side of the world! The day before we arrived in port my name was called out over the tannoy and so I reported to the staff sergeant, who told me to report to the railway station when we docked. There were about thirty-five Royal Engineers on board but I was the only one given 'movement papers'. On reaching the railway station I reported to a sergeant who issued me with a rifle and ammunition. He then informed me I would be going up country to Malaya. I asked him what the rifle was for and he told me I would be on guard duties on the train and some didn't come back from up country. Fuck me, I thought. I'd never heard of Malaya and certainly never heard of any trouble there! I had heard of trouble in Kenya with the Mau Mau and also with the Suez crisis. Apparently Malaya was in 'an emergency' as the government didn't want to call the 'troubles' war! The leader of the communist terrorists (C.T.) was called Chin Peng. I never really understood what it was all about and the emergency was practically over by the time I was there. Much of Malaya was covered in dense jungle and as I found out, was rich in rubber, with rubber plantations just about everywhere. There were only small pockets of C.T.s. operating and their leader, Chin Peng had been forced to retreat all the way up north to the south east Thai border. After travelling overnight on the train and standing guard (properly!) I eventually arrived at Kuala Lumpur where I was met by a driver in a Land Rover and taken to an army base, Batu-Contonment. My unit was 84 Field Survey Squadron and I was the new 'chippie'.

The lads were a mixed bunch of both regulars and National Service. Our living quarters were made of a basic wooden frame with a sort of thin thatch, leaf roof; the walls resembled a leaf screen and there was a doorway but no door! These buildings were called 'bashas'. The first thing that struck me when I got out of the Land Rover was the heat – it was so humid but I eventually found a basha with some spare beds.

In this basha, most of the occupied beds were all together at one end and just one occupied one right at the other end of the building, so I decided to take the bed next but one to the lone occupier.

That night I found out why it was so isolated and why the majority chose to stay together. I was fast asleep when this nut case woke me up. He was drunk and there was madness in his eyes. He was a big guy called John Mac. He started belting hell out of me. I ended up with two black eyes, a bust nose and a cut lip. The following day I thanked the lads for warning me and told them all that I might be able to do them a good turn one day. I decided my bed was staying put and when Mac came in drunk the next night, I was sat on the edge of my bed, facing his. He glared at me, grunted then fell fast asleep and I thought, 'Thank fuck!'

After I got over my sore face I joined the lads in the bar and we had some good laughs and good singalongs and I soon became known as someone good for a dare as I would try anything. I was always 'up for it'. Word had it that there was to be a visit to Batu Contonment by a bigwig general and so there was a lot of bull going on in the camp in preparation. The lads and I were in the bar trying to think of something to do to make the general feel welcome! It was suggested that I ride a bike, bollock naked, in front of the staff car that was transporting the top brass. The more we talked about it the more we laughed and so I agreed to do it. Come the day and the staff car was about fifty yards away, driving towards the officers' mess and I rode out in front of the car, arse in the air, pedalling like mad trying to keep my distance. I passed a line of officers who were waiting to meet the general and they looked as mad as hell at me, one captain reached out and tried to grab me which made me wobble. I fell off the bike! I leapt up and ran like mad; all the lads were whistling, cheering and generally falling about in fits of laughter. I got seven days in the nick for that stint but it was worth it. By now I was being talked about within the camp and Bully Mac was getting wary of me. I soon started to use the camp NAAFI and quickly joined in with all the camp boozers. Bully Mac was always challenging me to arm wrestle with him as he knew very well that he was able to beat me at that, but when he threw the gauntlet down for speed drinking pints of Tiger Beer I was always up for it and when he lost he was as mad as hell!

Bully Mac was the hard man of the camp and sooner or later he would 'have' anyone who was new. I just thought he was a nut case. He came from Glasgow with a reputation and he drank with a scouse lad who worked in the cook house and Scouse was his back up man. Scouse seemed alright to me but it always baffled me how so many lived in fear of so few. When a new lad was posted to join us I warned him about Bully Mac. He was a Yorkshire lad from Hull, called Cookie, and sure enough Mac was waiting for him. When another lad joined us both Cookie and I warned him about Mac and the three of us made a pact that we would stick together and kick the shit out of Bully Mac if he picked on us, any of us.

A few days later we were in the NAAFI and Mac was giving me the evil eye, I thought here we go, so I stood up and the lads I was with said not to do anything but I went over to his table and sat down. "What do you want?" he said. I told him what would happen to him if he went after the new lad and that if he thought nothing would happen to him if he beat me up again he was making a big mistake, because when he was asleep I would have him and it would be a lot worse than he gave me. He just turned to me and told me to fuck off, which I did. I had no idea as to what would happen next but tales got around the camp and rumour was that I was not someone to take liberties with.

It was about a week before my 19th birthday and a few of us had gone into Kuala Lumpur. We were in the B.B. Dance Hall; it was a great place with lots of girls that you could hire for a dance and there were some real beauties among them. We had a great night until we got a bit pissed and a fight broke out. The military police (M.Ps.) were sent for, I cracked one of them and when I woke up in a cell the next morning I couldn't remember anything that had happened until the charge was read out! I could not believe it. The M.P. said, 'When I went to apprehend who I now know to be Sapper Lettice, he struck me causing me to fall back and break a mirror. Lettice then said, 'Fuck off or I'll stick this knife between your fucking eyes!'" I interrupted him, saying that I didn't do things like that and that I thought he was making it out to be worse than it had been. I finished up being sentence to twenty-eight days detention, and was sent to a military prison called Kinrara. What a place that was. It was a prison of mixed military including army, navy, the R.A.F., Aussies, Kiwis, Gurkhas, and Malaysians. On admittance we were stripped searched whilst standing out in the open, on a grassed square bit of land and then had to bend over whilst they looked up our arses! So undignified! Everything was done at the double and it was run by staff sergeants who we had to address as 'Staff'. It was their job to try to break you. My first impression of the staff reminded me of the corporals at Chatham scrubbing the lad with hard bristle brush – mean, hard and bullies.

My first day was mind blowing. There was a mountain of sand which we had to shift from one end of the compound to the other. We did this by filling lead weight buckets and then carrying them one in each hand. It was knackering! And then when we had moved it all the bastards made us take it all back again! During my time at Kinrara I managed to keep out of trouble but as I was leaving one of the staff commented that I would be back. I didn't think there would be a cat in hell's chance of that! But he was right! He obviously saw something in me of which I was unaware.

On getting back to camp one or two of the lads had moved their beds closer to the other end of the room and nearer to my bed, which meant the fear of Mac was lifting!

After a few days in camp I was told I was going into the jungle with a surveyor to do some map making of the area and that we had six days to complete the task. We had a local tribesman as a guide and two Gurkhas who were radio operators. We travelled down river in a boat called *The State of Johore*, then in some remote area, we disembarked and, with all our gear, off we marched in a line into the jungle. The guide was in front, then the surveyor, the two Gurkhas next and then me riding shotgun. We had only ventured about three hundred yards when we heard a great noise and then something came crashing through the undergrowth. The guide started first to shout and then to run like mad. We all swiftly followed suit but without knowing why! It soon became apparent though, because we just made it back to the boat when a massive rhino appeared on the river bank. There it was, this huge great mean looking snorting animal. I stared at it in amazement I had no idea such animals were in the jungles of Malaya. We still had a job to do and so, hoping the rhino was long gone, we found another place to moor up and start the trek off into the jungle again. The Gurkhas were great, they made somewhere for us to sleep each night before they made their own sleeping area and the guide also kept a look out for me, knowing that I was a novice in the jungle. He stopped me one time from touching what I thought to be a glorious flower: he pulled me back, poked it with a stick; it was a snake! I learnt quite a lot from those six days of jungle life and the only thing that I really didn't like were the leeches, they were such awful things. When our task was finished we left the jungle and travelled down the river to a rubber plantation where we were to be picked up by army personnel. The manager of the plantation got very excited when we told him about the rhino. It turned out to be the first sighting of one for six years. I felt very privileged and boy, did we have a tale to tell back at camp. I enjoyed my time in Kuala Lumpur and even my time in Kinrara, as it hadn't really bothered me much and I had met some great lads from all over the Far East whilst being there.

Back in camp the commanding officer, Major Parr, was going back to Blighty (the U.K.) and he asked me to make him a dozen wooden crates with his name and home address stencilled on them. I did the best job I could because he was an OK bloke and I quite liked him. When I had finished them he thanked me and told me he would leave me a drink behind the bar in the NAAFI. That drink turned out to be fifty dollars! Brilliant. We had a party before he left held in the squadron compound. Everybody came, including wives.

I was looking forward to a good night and I was determined not to get drunk. It started off a bit slow but as the married pads arrived things started to pick up and it was good to dance with some British women again. I was sat with my mates, telling jokes and bragging about what we could do with one or two of the women when two corporals and their wives came in and sat down about five yards away from us. As one of the wives sat down she looked across at our table and I smiled! She was about twenty eight or thirty, good looking and slim. Our eyes met – just a casual glance, but it was enough for me. I couldn't stop myself from looking at her, hoping our eyes would meet again, which they did and after a while I plucked up the courage to ask her to dance. She looked at her husband, who in turn looked up at me and he sort of nodded to her. When we danced she asked me my name and when I told her she said, "Oh, I've heard about you!" I asked her what her name was and when she said it was Ellie I said, "Oh, I've heard about *you*." She laughed and said that there wasn't much to hear. I said I didn't believe that for one second. As we danced I noticed that she was about three inches shorter than I was, that she had fair hair, green eyes, was wearing a loose cotton dress and that she smelt lovely. She told me that she had been in Malaya for about eighteen months and that she was looking forward to going home in six months time. I told her a few stories about what had been going back in Blighty. I liked Ellie, thanked her for dancing with me and was about to return her to where her husband was sitting, when a 'smoochie' record of Conway Twitty's, *It's Only Make Believe*, started playing. It immediately reminded me of Joe Mort's place in Accrington. Ellie and I danced really slowly as I said to her, "That's what this is, only make believe." She moved closer to me, put her head on my shoulder and her arms around my neck. We just seemed to stand on the same spot for ages and I could feel her pressing her body up to mine. I was unable to stop myself from rising to the occasion! I was desperate to kiss her but stopped myself. Ellie lifted her head and looking at me full on, said, "Who's a naughty boy then?" I made a quick glance towards her husband to see if he had been watching and was relieved to see he was busy talking. Ellie must have read my thoughts and said that he wouldn't have noticed anything at all. I watched her as she went back to her husband and whispered something in his ear after which they both laughed. Ellie glanced across at me with a faint smile on her lovely face. I don't know why but I started to feel a little uncomfortable, but then I shrugged my shoulders and thought, 'What the hell.'

By the end of the night I had danced with most of the wives including Mrs Parr, the C.O's. wife. She was a real lady and spoke very nicely saying that she had very much enjoyed her time in Malaya and wished they were staying longer. She said that her husband had mentioned me to her but that having met me, I wasn't at all as she had expected. I had no answer to that!

After I had returned her to the major I shook his hand, wishing him all the best on his return home. He, in return, thanked me for doing a good job on his wooden crates and suggested I try to stay out of trouble. He told me that if I could stop drinking so much I had the makings of a good soldier and that I had certain qualities to be a leader. Yeah, I thought to myself, wished him goodbye and good luck and went back to camp. I lay in bed thinking what a great night it had been and why things couldn't be like that every day? The next day: reality! It was getting towards tea time when a group of about twenty men turned up to be fed. I say men because that is what they seemed compared to us lads. They looked rough and they turned out to be tough as well as rough! They were the S.A.S and had been up country near to the Thai border for a month. After they were fed they took over theNAAFI. What a night! I joined them and by the end of the night I also joined them in a dancing ceremony which was called *The dance of the flaming arseholes*. This dance comprised us lining up, dropping our pants and bending over. A piece of paper was rolled up into the shape of a cone, inserted up the arse and then set fire to. The person whose paper burned to the shortest length won! We did this whilst dancing to Connie Francis singing *Who's sorry now?* I didn't win but I did burn my arse in the trying and which I proudly displayed to one and all! The S.A.S had gone by morning.

A few weeks had passed without my getting into trouble when a few of us went for a night out into Kuala Lumpar and whilst out, we bumped into the corporal whose wife I had danced with, Ellie. He was with a couple of his mates and they joined us. I supposed he wasn't too bad, for an N.C.O. Towards the end of the night we went for a curry and after we finished eating we just messed about, had a laugh and had a bit of a sing song. It was a great night and there had been no trouble. The corporal's name was Ray and before he left for home he suggested that I should have a weekend at his place. I asked him what his wife would have to say about that and he said, "Nothing, you know her anyway from the party," so I just replied "OK, why not!"

The following week, on the Friday, he arrived at my quarters to pick me up and told me to take some 'civvies' with me and that we could get changed at his place. Ray told me all the married 'pads' had a drink together at the weekends and so I was looking forward to it.

When we arrived his wife, Ellie, looked at me as if to say, What are you doing here? It was a look that made me think Ray hadn't told her about my visit. She seemed very cool towards me and she kept giving Ray dirty looks and so when she took me to show me where to put my things I whispered, "I'm sorry, Ellie. I thought he told you he had invited me."

"No, he didn't," she replied, "but not to worry, enjoy yourself, I'll get you a beer". Ray joined me and we had a beer together and he told me that some of their friends would be joining us later. Ellie than joined me whilst Ray went off to get changed. I wasn't a hundred percent comfortable about the situation, but she did look great and so I told her that I thought she looked lovely and I apologised for being there and said that I had assumed that Ray would have told her that he had invited me to stay. She thanked me and said, "My husband tells me very little but he has told me about you. Is it true you were naked, riding a bike, when the general arrived in camp?" I laughed and told her I was guilty but that I had just wanted to give him a warm welcome. She said that she would have liked to have seen that but I told her that it was not a pretty sight, but if that had been her on the bike that would have been a different thing and what a wonderful vision that would have been. She giggled and told me that the 'top brass' had actually thought it had been funny too. By the time Ray joined us again I felt more relaxed and I thought Ellie was too. By the time I had showered and changed their friends had arrived, bringing lots of booze and some food. I saw that I was by far the youngest at only nineteen but by the time we all had a few drinks I felt fine. My name came up once or twice, with the naked bike ride story getting funnier by the minute. Then the episode of the rhino was told with lots of questions asked and comments of 'brilliant' made. Not so brilliant was the story of the fight with the military police but I didn't see that I was as bad a person as some of them were making me out to be, but anyway, another beer and a change of subject. When everyone had a good drink inside them we had a sing song and my party piece was *Great Balls of Fire* which was very well received! Then it was all over and goodnights were said. Ray told me that he was glad he had asked me over and that he had enjoyed the night and I told him that I had too. When I awoke the next morning everywhere was very quiet and I had no idea of the time so I had a shower, slipped on a pair of shorts and went into the kitchen. I was just about to get a drink of water when I spotted Ellie in the garden hanging out some washing and, oh, what a lovely sight she was too. She was wearing a white cotton dress which, in the sunlight, was see through and as she started walking back to the house I couldn't help but stare: she appeared not to be wearing any underwear! When she came in the kitchen and said, "Good morning," I'm sure my face must have been very red! She told me that Ray was out playing cricket but not to worry because she would take me back to camp. She made some breakfast and we sat opposite each other at the table. We were alone and I was struggling to make small talk, but managed to mutter that I had enjoyed the night and that I thought her pals were OK! She told me that they thought I was good for a laugh and that she was glad that I had been there. It was then, when she got up to make us some coffee, that I noticed the top button and the two bottom buttons of her dress were undone. When she sat down again I told her that the only thing missing the previous night had been a smoochie dance and, smiling, she said, "Well, you never know." I was stumped then and did a typical school boy trick and dropped my teaspoon on the floor. I bent down to pick it up and fuck me, there she sat with her legs slightly apart, so that I could see just about everything usually hidden! My face must have been blood red when I sat back in the chair but Ellie looked me straight in the eyes and said, "Did you find what you were looking for?" Whilst I was struggling as to what to do or say Ellie stood up, cleared the table and started to do the washing up. I then stood up and, offering to dry the pots, I walked up behind her. I just couldn't contain myself any longer and I put my arms around her waist and there was no protest as I moved my hands slowly up her body to cup her breasts. Ellie pushed her lovely bottom back into me and gave out a little murmur as I pinched her now hardened nipples and she then turned her head sideways and kissed me passionately. I had, by this time, become an almost dithering wreck but at the same time was desperate not to mess things up.. She pushed back onto me and said, "It's OK, Jimmy." I couldn't believe what had just happened! Ellie kissed me and went into the bathroom. She reappeared a minute later, her white dress was completely open and she looked magnificent. She cleaned me with a flannel and we started kissing again: then, taking me by the hand, she led me into my bedroom. She stripped me and then removed her dress. What a body, a real woman.

Ellie lay on her back and with her knees raised and legs parted, she pulled me down on top of her. Our lips touched very softly and very gently at first and then our kisses became more and more passionate until I thought her tongue couldn't possibly go any deeper into my mouth. We made love again, slowly this time and she very skilfully taught me and showed me what pleased her and she certainly knew how to please me, but I think she was still surprised when, later as we talked, she asked me how old I was, I told her nineteen!

She smiled at me, I told her I told her that I had just spent my nineteenth birthday in Kinrara and she seemed a little surprised asking, "Is that all you are? Do you know how old I am?" But I told her not to tell me because I had an age for her in my head and that was the age I saw her as. She then told me that as soon as she saw me the day before, she had thought that this would happen and I confessed that after we had danced at the party, I had masturbated once I had got back and gone to bed but I would never have dreamed of what had just happened between us. We just lay there, holding hands and talking then I turned on my side, and kissing her said, "I think I can truly say that without any shadow of doubt that I am now a member of 'the well and truly done' club!" Ellie looked at me, smiled and said, as she started to fondle me again, "Well, not quite yet!" Bloody hell, she was one hell of a woman. She said that she wished Ray would look at her the way I looked at her, which surprised me because I couldn't understand him not wanting to be shagging her day in and day out! She

71

told me that things between them hadn't been too good of late and that she had really needed what had happened between us. We started to laugh about the day and particularly me dropping the spoon! I gave her gorgeous bottom a little spank, followed by a play fight, then Ellie straddled me and taking hold of my hands, started to slowly move forwards and backwards, just wriggling about. Alas, I was unable to rise to the occasion, I was aching and I was a spent force! It didn't seem to put her off and she slowly managed to get me a little harder, then she released my hands at her breasts and I tweaked her nipples. How she was able to orgasm again was beyond me. I felt as though I had been initiated and had come of age!

Like all good things in life, it had to come to end sometime and it was time for me to leave. I went for a shower and got dressed whilst Ellie changed the bed. I looked at her and smiled and she got me a cold can of Tiger beer from the fridge, telling me to wait for her in the garden. A friend of Ellie's waved to me from the road, saying that last night had been a good night. It certainly had. I must have been grinning like a Cheshire cat as Ellie came out. "I know what you're smiling about," she said. "I feel the same." Then all of a sudden I thought of Ray and a feeling of guilt came over me. Ellie assured me our secret was safe with her and that she wouldn't be telling anyone, and she asked me not to go bragging to my mates. I promised I wouldn't and she thanked me for that. It was a promise I kept. "Right, Jimmy lad, let's get you back to camp." I looked at her and thought, wow, gorgeous. We got into the car and her dress rode up her thighs. "I can see you have got your panties on now." She laughed. "Yes, but my plan worked, didn't it?" I ran my hand up the inside of her smooth thighs; she smiled and touched my hand. Then we were on our way. We talked a lot on the journey and I was a bit taken aback when she mentioned her kids. It had never entered my head! She had two boys, eight and six, and she said she would love a baby girl and would maybe try again. It entered my head that she may not have to try too hard after what had just happened! The boys were away with some other children, camping in the Cameron Highlands. The next thing we were back at camp and I took hold of her hand saying, "Thank you,

Ellie," and she replied that the pleasure had been all hers. I would have loved to have kissed but held back as we didn't want to be seen. It was the last time I saw Ellie.

When I got back to the basha (billet) the lads started to ask me how it had gone, but I just said that it had been OK, that there hadn't been any trouble, nobody had taken the piss, that we had a few laughs and a bit of a sing song and that it had been a good night. They asked about Ray's wife because they had known about the dance at the party. I told them that was the only thing missing: no dance! I was shattered and told the lads not to waken me before tea. I fell asleep with a smile on my face and that night I made an excuse not to go out with the lads into Kuala Lumpur but instead I went into the NAAFI for a couple of drinks. I bumped into Ray a few days later. I felt guilty as I spoke to him, especially when he told me he had enjoyed the night and that maybe we could do that again sometime. I knew that wouldn't happen but just told him, "That would be nice."

I had been in Malaya about six months and had managed to settle down. I had stayed out of trouble since the stay with Ray and Ellie and even Bully Mac was no longer a problem. I was happy just to go to the NAAFI, have a few drinks then back to bed, and just to get drunk occasionally. I was sent to the Cameron Highlands for a seven day retreat. It was high in the mountains where the old colonials used to retreat to in the height of summer. It was a cool place that looked a little like England and had red telephone boxes, red post boxes and one place up there looked like a great country house that served homemade scones with jam and cream and pots of tea. How very English. I started to look above my head, I was sure there would be a halo there! On my return to base camp I found out that I was going back into the jungle. This time there were to be two surveyors and I was again to be riding shotgun. We had carried enough supplies for the five days allocated for the job. We had completed the job and we were making our way out of the jungle when our compass started to go haywire. We were in an anti-magnetic field and we were unable to get our bearings! The food ran out but we did have some curry powder left. Everything that moved got curried! We had been lost for three days when luckily for us we were spotted by a search party made up of Ghurkhas.

They guided us to them by firing shots into the air and we responded by doing the same. It was a great feeling to meet up with the Ghurkhas and there was a lot of hand shaking and much thanking. They said they would inform the camp as to where to pick us up, then they pointed us in the direction of a rubber plantation and we were left to our own devices again. Our compasses were once more in working order and so off we went to the plantation. We arrived in complete darkness and were looking forward to some good food and drink. Alas, it wasn't to be. We couldn't find the plantation owner and as we were knackered, we decided to have a kip in the longhouse where the rubber tappers stayed. We went in but again, nobody there. We climbed the ladder up to where the workers slept, found a quiet comer and fell asleep. I woke up to the sound of excitable voices below, I thought they must have been talking about us and so I crept over to take a look. All the workers were gathered around the fire and in the middle were two men with rifles. I could just make out a red star on their hats so it was certain that they were C.Ts. (terrorists). Some of the workers were telling them to go and I crawled back to the lads and whispered what was going on. Whilst I got my rifle and ammunition ready, they crawled over to sneak a look for themselves. A lot more chatter went on around the fire and then eventually the C.Ts. left. We stayed where we were for about five minutes and then we made our way down the ladder. The workers were startled and I think some were even frightened and so as we approached them I put my finger over my lips, indicating to them to be quiet.

We made our way up to the big house where the plantation owner made us very welcome, but he was surprised when we told him about the terrorists. He told us that there hadn't been any trouble in that area for quite a while. He phoned the police straight away and when they arrived we told them of what we knew and they then grilled the workers for information. The C.Ts. had apparently been looking for new recruits. Our driver eventually arrived to take us back to camp and within hours everybody was talking about our little escapade. As I had been riding shotgun I cracked on that of course I would have blown their fucking heads off if the C.Ts.

had started. In truth I was relieved nothing happened. That was as near as I ever came to active service!

I started getting into more trouble again. I suppose I was just a plain nuisance. I would get drunk most nights and would do stupid things, but during the day I would be OK and if I was given something to do I would always make sure that I did it to the best of my ability. The night was different: I would refuse orders, go AWOL (absent without leave) and get so drunk that the next day I wouldn't be able to remember what had happened. One time the guard woke me up because my bed had been on fire! I had fallen asleep with a cigarette in my hand! The guard had thrown water over me, the bedding and the mattress. Apparently I just staggered outside, had a pee under a palm tree and went back inside where the guard showed me what I had done. I said, "Fucking hell," and climbed back into what was left of the bed and went back to sleep.

Next morning I was as black as hell and I stank of smoke. More stoppage of pay!

I had spent my 19th birthday in prison and was about to spend my 20th birthday in the same place. My name was down to do guard duty but I decided that I would have a night out in Kuala Lumpur instead and whilst out I had bumped into Ray, who told me that I should go back to camp, but I just replied, "Guck that for a game of soldiers, I'll wait to be picked up." I asked him how his wife was and he told me that she was great but that she would be disappointed to find that I was still getting into trouble. He told me that they were to return to Blighty the following week. I just wished him good luck and we went our separate ways. I had been AWOL for a couple of days when the military police eventually picked me up. I was sentenced to twenty eight days in Kinrara. The staff who had said to me previously that I would be back was still there and of course he recognised me and gave me a knowing look. I knew the script and swapped my gear with someone who was getting out. The gear he gave to me looked like it had been in Kinrara for years! Poor chap. I did my time without any problems occurring, it was after all only 28 days.

As I was leaving the same staff said the same thing to me, that I would be back. I just wondered what it was he could see in me that I couldn't see in myself and so I asked him and he just said it was the drink! Cheeky sod, I thought. He went on to ask me what the first thing I did was when I was inside the prison. I just shrugged my shoulders and he said that I volunteered to give blood so that I could get the can of beer given to all donors and then I would volunteer to clean up the staff club so that I could drink the dregs out of the dirty glasses. "You'll be back."

My days in 84 Field Survey Squadron were numbered after I cracked a guy who was thieving from the lockers. I caught him, thumped him and then chased him as far as the guard room, where he asked the guard to lock him up for his own safety! I was posted two days later, destination Singapore. I was given my movement papers, a rail pass and then caught the overnight train in Kuala Lumpur. I spent most of my time in the buffet bar but did manage to get some sleep before arriving next morning in Singapore. It was a late in the day on the Saturday when I eventually made my way to Gillman

Barracks but I didn't bother reporting in to anyone, instead I went straight to the NAAFI, where I met a couple of the lads and that was that! We were well and truly pissed by the end of the night, when a bit of trouble started and the guards were called out, along with a couple of regimental police (R.P.) We were escorted to the guard room where the Sergeant of Guard was there to greet us. The guard commander walked up to me and asked me my name, I told him and he replied, "So you are Lettice, are you?" I had just travelled over 700 miles and my name had gone before me. I couldn't work that one out, I was only a young lad from Blackpool, not some hard case. I was again locked up for the night and the following morning an officer came to see me his words were, "So you're Lettice. Wwell, you won't be staying at Gillman Barracks." He looked at my movement papers, signed them and dismissed me. I was now on my way to Borneo. Where's Borneo? I thought!

I left Gillman Barracks on the Sunday morning with no travel pass and very little money. I had been told that I had to find my own way to Borneo and once there to report to 11 Independent Field Squadron. I made my way to Singapore's famous Bugis Street, where there were plenty of girls looking for business. I started chatting and having a laugh with some of them communicating in pidgin English, such as, 'You, me, jig-a-jig'. I had also learnt enough Malay language to say, 'Ber appa ringit satu mala?' It meant, 'how much one night?' The girls had such wonderful names such as Juicy Lucy, Diamond Lil and Suzie Lu and because they plied their trade openly they were thought of as being hard, but I found most of them had a real big heart.

They knew I was in trouble and they tried to help. One of them went into a nearby bar whilst I stood outside waiting for her. A few minutes later she pulled me inside, sat me down, gave me a bottle of Anchor beer and a Chinese man brought me a dish of food and motioned to me to eat. Her name was Annie and she was with a half a dozen navy lads. She was going to do well with these lads, they were off the *Ark Royal* and had just arrived, fresh, white faced and with lots of money in their back pockets which the girls were intending to have a share of. After a few minutes a couple of 'matleos' came over to my table asking where my mates were. I told them that the girls were my mates but that I was trying to get to Borneo and by the way, where was Borneo? They started to laugh and then they invited me to join them. It was a rare event for army and navy lads to drink together but I joined them and their pals and the booze was flowed freely. Stories were told with each one trying to outdo the other and when they asked me how I managed to end up in Singapore on my own, trying to thumb a lift to Borneo, they were well impressed and they seemed to think I was hilarious. Annie walked into the bar to see how I was and when she saw me in the middle of all these matleos she said, "Ha you okey dokey?" I went over to her, took her hand, saying, "Thank you, Annie, you my friend." The navy lads knew I was skint so they took me on a tour of Singapore and then, just before going back to their ship, they had a whip round for me. How great was that? I went to the docks with them to see if there was any merchant vessel I could cadge a lift off but unfortunately there was none. I did however get invited on board a Dutch ship for a drink and some food and a bed for the night. The next morning the captain said I should try Changi airport and he too laughed when I asked him where Borneo was. He showed me on the map where it was and I declared, "That's not too bad, I could swim there!" The crew wished me luck and away I went. I could see the *Ark Royal* in the distance and gave it a salute, saying out loud, "Thank you, lads." I went back to the bar in Bugis Street to collect my gear. I thanked the bar owner but was unable to find Annie. It was too early for the girls, they would need all the rest they could get before business started again.

I got a trishaw to Changi airport, which was a fair distance away and when I got there I simply walked round the airfield, asking if anyone was taking a plane to Borneo. It seemed they were going everywhere but! Australia, Hong Kong, India – and then someone suggested I try the cargo plane about two hundred yards away. I found the pilot, who seemed a like a great guy: an Aussie by the name of Bruce, and yes, he was going to Borneo. He was as rough as hell but I liked him straight away and when I asked him for a lift he just said, "Sure," but that I would have to sit next to him in the cockpit. "Great" I said.

A couple of hours later I was following him and climbing up some slats on the side of the plane to get into the cockpit. The seat I had was just like a dining chair that had been fixed to the floor! The plane itself had four engines and huge propellers. Take off was pretty shaky to say the least, but we managed to get airborne and it was goodbye, Singapore!

The flight was superb and the sights were wonderful, with lots of tropical islands covered in lush green jungle, surround by white sands and turquoise seas. Bruce and I spent the time chatting and he told me that there was just him and his partner that ran the business and so they were, to some extent, free to make their own decisions. I thought how brilliant that was. He asked me how I came to be thumbing a lift to Borneo and after I told him some of my escapades he asked how old I was. I was just twenty! "Blimey, mate, you've caused a lot of trouble for one so young," was his comment. It made me stop talking and do some thinking.

It didn't seem that long ago that I had been just an ordinary kid, not a care in the world, just having fun with my pals but look at me now! I had been in a military prison twice, spent lots of time in the guard room, had a bad reputation and on top of that, I had been on what seemed like permanent stoppage of pay! I felt I had done some good things though. Well, I did a good job when I was in the jungle. So yes, Bruce was right when I looked back, I had done quite a lot over the last two years.

We eventually reached Borneo and landed at Jesstleton which was the capital of British North Borneo. I shook hands with Bruce, thanking him for the lift. He told me it had been a pleasure; he wished me luck and said for me to try to keep out of trouble. We then went our separate ways.

Jesstleton only had two main roads and so I hung about in a bar/hotel waiting for a lift, but knowing I could get a bed there if needed. I sat near the saloon-type swing doors so that I could see any vehicles that came along. I had only been there about an hour when an army Land Rover drove down the road. I stepped out and it pulled up and stopped for me. I asked the driver if he knew where I might find 11 Independent and he told me to jump in. He said the 11th was stationed about sixty miles north and that he was picking up the mail first, but would then take me there and so by the time we arrived at the camp, it was dark. The sergeant major showed me where the cook house was and where I could sleep, he then told me that we would get everything else sorted in the morning.

I went straight to the NAAFI for a drink, where I got myself a can of Tiger beer. I had just sat down when a fight broke out. I saw a few punches being thrown and then one of the lads ran past me, chased by a nut case brandishing a 'gollock' (a large knife). He swung the gollock at the young lad, missed him but got it stuck in the tent pole. The young lad saw his opportunity and smacked the chaser in the nose. There was blood everywhere and I was thinking, Blimey, what sort of place had I been sent to? It wasn't long of course before I joined in the fun of trying to out drink one another but it started to get a bit silly when after the beer came the spirits. I downed half a pint of whisky in one then somebody else downed a pint of whisky and then a complete 'barm pot' downed a pint of whiskey followed by a pint of rum. I saw him collapse and later found out that he had very nearly died. The next morning I was up before the commanding officer, who was looking through my movement papers but asking me where I had been since I'd left Kaula Lumpar on the Sunday. I told him that I hadn't been given any travel documents and so I had to find my own way to Borneo. He then looked up and me and said, "Well, Lettice, it seems that Kuala Lumur didn't want you, Singapore refused to have you and we don't want you here with us either. We have got our commonwealth friends here and so you will be going to join 1 Troop in the field later today." I thought, 'Where the fuck to now!'

A driver came to pick me up and I was on my way again. We passed through a little Kampong town called Kota Belud and drove on down to a river. We crossed over the river using a ferry which had been built by and operated by the Aussies and the road leading up on the other side of the river was being built by the Brits. It was uphill and all very dodgy to negotiate but we eventually arrived at camp where there were just seven tents for accommodation, a large tent for the cookhouse and in the distance, perched on top of a mountain, was the NAAFI tent. This tent was only big enough for two tables and four benches. There were some piss heads in that place, I can tell you. I found an empty bed in one of the tents, where I left my gear and then asked a corporal who to see and what to do. He didn't seem to know and I wasn't bothered, I was knackered so I just lay on top of the bed. When I woke up it was dinner time and the lads had returned from work. The lad who had the bed next to mine asked me my name and told me his was Paul, then, "That's Ian over there, Paddy and Lofty." I raised my hand to them all went and had some dinner with them and then off to work for the afternoon, where I got to know a few more of the lads and I thought to myself that the place was alright. At the end of the day it was a shower and change, something to eat and then the lads said they were off to the NAAFI and was I joining them? I still had some of the money left that the navy lads had given me but as I didn't know when I would next get any pay I was hesitant to go with them, plus I was thinking, 'Drink and trouble'!

I was getting a little bit fed up of just being moved from camp to camp. I tossed it about in my head for a moment or two then thought, 'Oh, bollocks to it, let's go'. The bar was about eight-foot-long with a foot rest at the bottom of it. There was a sign painted above the foot rest that read, 'Please mind your head': apparently someone had slid down off the bar and then cut his head on the foot rest as he was getting back up, pissed of course! The tables were on a slight slope and there was a thick white line painted the whole length of the table. What we did was to place the empty beer can on the line: it would then roll down the whole length of the table, out of the tent and disappear down the mountain, brilliant. After a few cans of Tiger I needed a pee and Ian pointed to a flap in the tent. It was pitch black outside; I had only taken two strides when I too disappeared down the mountain. It took me ages to climb back up to the tent, where all the lads were cheering and falling about laughing. I just shouted, "Bastards," and sat down again. I had to wait a few weeks before a new lad arrived; I was just busting to tell him where the toilet was.

The morning after the night before, as usual I had wet the bed but by now, I was well used to it and didn't feel the shame that I should have felt, and so very blatantly, I dragged my mattress outside to dry in the sun and then put it back on my bed after work. When we were in the NAAFI tent that night, someone asked who the dirty bastard was who put his mattress outside to dry. Of course I owned up as being that dirty bastard and said that it was better than getting into a wet bed. Nobody commented! The next morning when I put my mattress outside three others appeared and within a week there must have been ten mattresses each morning, lying outside with steam rising from all of them. I'd started something here! The stench was getting bad and a sergeant decreed that there was to be a mattress inspection and the following morning I woke up to a noise which sounded like a bed being pulled across the floor. It was Paul Broon trying desperately to roll up his mattress. He was having a right old tussle.

The mattresses were made of straw and he had wet his bed so many times that the mattress had rusted to the springs. As he pulled the mattress it split open and the filling spilled out! He was seen running down the mountain with a can of petrol, a lighter and the remains of a mattress. All that was left for the inspection were some rusty old springs with bits of straw stuck to them.

He was the one who asked who the dirty bastard was who put his mattress outside! I gave him some stick for a long time but it was like water off a duck's back. He just laughed it off. Paul, Ian, Charlie, Kinch and I all became really good pals.

The work that we were doing was mainly road building, plus the making of an airstrip but I was asked to build some toilets: proper ones, not just some holes in the ground. At that moment I thought I had reached the pinnacle of my career in the army, A Bog Builder. We had some timber brought in and then I dug a good long, deep trench. I built six open air toilets. I used thick canvas for the walls, making them a little more private and each toilet had a wooden lid over the hole. I thought I had done a really good job and felt a certain sense of satisfaction, especially when the lads said how great they were. I had started to enjoy where we were camped. The first thing that I saw each morning was a great view of Mount Kinabulu. It was the highest mountain in South East Asia and often shrouded in swirling clouds. The second thing I saw as I came out of the tent was a long line of women on their way to the paddy fields. They all carried long knives and they were always dressed in black. They were of the Duson tribe. Late one night one of these women came into the camp. She was badly injured and her arm was hanging off. The medic tried to patch her up but she really needed hospital treatment, so we strapped her into the back of a Land Rover and then the medic and the medic's pal drove off down the mountain. Jessleton was the only place with a hospital and it was two hours away from camp. We were in the middle of the monsoon season so the weather was terrible, with torrential rain and it was a pitch black night. They were about halfway into the journey at a point on the river where there was a concrete bridge. This bridge had no sides and no railings and the river was a torrent. The medic was feeling his way over the bridge with the aim of guiding the driver and Land Rover across. Very tragically, they were all swept away and were drowned. We found the bodies two days later down river, the Duson tribeswoman still strapped into the back of the Land Rover. What a sad time that was. We never even knew her name.

Time passed by and eventually our spirits lifted and we were back to laughing, working and of course, getting drunk. Ian always made me smile, he was one of the gang and he came from Leven in Scotland. He had no front teeth and so he would always cover his mouth with his hand when he laughed. As he was so self-conscious about having no teeth, he had some false ones made but when they arrived and he put them in and smiled, they made him look rather like a camel. Not long after he got his teeth we gave the NAAFI a miss and we went into Kota Belud instead. We all clambered on to a dumper truck, having to hold on for dear life as it bounced about over the dirt track. When we arrived we parked the truck on the grass, went into the double fronted bar and started to drink.

We very soon became entertainment for the locals who sat cross-legged on the grass, just watching us as we sang, laughed, got drunk and fell over. I suppose we must have looked like the idiots that they thought we were. At the end of the night it was back into the truck and another bumpy ride as we made our drunken way back to camp. We had just managed to cross the river and to pick up speed along the track when, bang, we hit a great hole in the track. Unfortunately Ian's newly acquired teeth shot out of his mouth, never to be seen again! It was back to hand over mouth. He was gutted, he only had them for two days. He had waited three months for his choppers but they were gone in a flash.

I was in Borneo for seven months and, apart from the awful time when some of our lads drowned, I enjoyed every minute of my time there, although I had often wondered, if I had been with them whether I would have been as brave as they had been. Anyway the only real trouble that I got myself into was when I went AWOL for a few days in Jesstleton. Whilst there I 'copped' for a young lady of ill repute and so I stayed on and booked myself a room in a rather ramshackle hotel. I then let the room for a small fee to any of the squaddies that turned up: that way I earned a few extra bob for beer money. A couple of the lads from my lot arrived and stayed for a couple of days and when it was time for them to return I decided to go back with them and to face the music. I knew there was no guard room or anything like that there. All that happened to me that time was fourteen days' stoppage of pay and a short confinement to camp. It was hardly punishment really as I still got pissed every night, courtesy of the lads. When it was time for us to leave Borneo we piled into trucks and were driven to Jessleton. As we passed the locals they waved to us and I wondered if it was a wave of good riddance, or simply goodbye. The airfield at Jessleton was pretty basic, to say the least, with just one runway and a large wooden hut where we sat waiting for the plane to arrive. We saw it approach and we watched as it attempted to land, it hit the ground and bounced about sixty feet back into the air! The plane, a Hastings, did this about five or six times before it came to a halt. We boarded in fear and trepidation and as the plane took off it shook and shuddered, but at last we became airborne and were safely on our way back to Malaya.

We landed at Butterworth and the camp we joined was 11 Independent Field Squadron. There was another camp next to ours where there was an attachment of Aussies and it was at that camp that I met up again with an old school pal called Mick Molloy. The two camps were practically on the beach, with coconut trees all around and directly facing the beach was the island of Penang.

I was dead happy to see Mick; he looked really well and was working as a plant operator. He said he had heard a few tales about me and asked if they were true. "Sort of," I said to which he replied that he thought I was a bit of a bugger and like it or not, I had got myself a bad reputation. Within just a few days of arriving at Butterworth we were on our way up north to the jungle to do more road building. Our job was to do a month in the jungle and then another troop would take over. This suited me fine because it allowed me to catch up with my stoppages of pay, which seemed to have been a permanent feature during my time in the army. After cutting away a load of dense undergrowth we managed to set up camp on a hillside, building a very basic sleeping area which had a ground sheet slung above our hammocks. We lived off the food rations which we had taken with us into the jungle, plus some fresh food which the RAF parachuted in to us once a week and for which we were very grateful. To enable them to do this we made a bit of a clearing and tied a large orange balloon to the tallest tree. When the pilot saw the balloon they would make the drop. We were each given a number by the N.C.O. and so if I was number six I had to retrieve the sixth parachute dropped. Simple, until a parachute got caught in a tree! Still, at least we were allowed to keep the parachute, which made lovely shirts or perhaps a hammock. We cooked our food in a mess tin and many a time we shared it with any ants or creepy crawlies that had managed to climb in. They would all just get mixed in with the rice pudding or whatever we were cooking and then eaten. It was just extra protein. We would also receive cigarettes, mainly Woodbines, which were in sealed tins of fifty per tin. Then there was the rum, the *creme de la creme* of the drop. This arrived in large flagons and was portioned out every night. There were about ten of us that drank the rum out of thirty two. The ones that didn't want it just gave us their ration. That was a lot of rum. The ten of us would sit around the fire at night having a laugh, drinking and getting very pissed. Our days were mainly spent cutting through the jungle, usually by hand or, where there were large rocks or trees, we would use plastic explosives. I really enjoyed this time in the army and I believed I proved myself in lots of ways and would push myself forward when problems arose. Volunteering, however, could sometimes have a down side, like the time when the lads ran away from a swarm of hornets and I stepped forward to deal with it. The nest was right in the path that we were making and so I decided to smoke them out just like with bees! Somehow though it didn't quite work and instead of calming them, it made them extremely cross and I ended up staggering blindly about, having been stung all over my face, lips and eyes, everywhere that wasn't covered up. It took quite a while to recover but it did teach me not to volunteer for anything unless I knew what I was doing.

When our month was up and we returned to base camp at Butterworth, the lads would all collect their five weeks' pay whilst I would collect five weeks' half pay! We would then tart ourselves up and, 'Penang, here we come'. It was a ferry across to the island then a trishaw to the NAAFI club, where we would get pissed; we would then head off down to Love Lane and to the brothels. The Sing Tong Lom was our favourite, we would have a good laugh, a good shag, and on the odd occasion the girls would even let me have it on tick! My favourite was called Doya, she was a Malay girl who had got herself pregnant. Her family had disowned her and, because she felt she had no other means to support herself or her baby, she had turned to prostitution. She wasn't as brash or as brassy as the other girls and I felt sorry for her having been cut off from her family. Penang was certainly a fabulous island and we would go there every weekend unless we were in the jungle, or in my case, unless I was locked up in the guard house. Yes, I had started to get into trouble again and once it started it just didn't seem to stop. One time I was given fourteen days' detention for losing my rifle and ammunition. I was on guard duty but instead of patrolling the camp I patrolled the NAAFI, but before going in for a drink I did manage to hide my rifle. This was all well and good until the guard commander came looking for me, by which time I was so drunk I couldn't remember where I had hidden it. I came to in the cells with the corporal saying, "For fucks sake just tell me where you left your rifle and your ammunition." Both the camps were out looking for it and eventually it was found under a mattress, on a bed in the other camp where the Aussies were. The Aussies were a little bit older than we were and they thought they were just a little bit better than us, which of course didn't go down well and meant that trouble was never very far away. When the booze was flowing the insults would start, they would call us pommie bastards and we would reply with, "Fuck off back to where you came from," that sort of childish thing. Then fists would fly, a mass brawl would start and a great time was had by all. The Aussies would come over to our NAAFI a few nights later and it would be a repeat performance. On one of these events I bit off more than I could chew when an Aussie asked me to go outside, just me and him. Well, of course I had to take him up on his kind offer but after I had hit him a couple of times to no effect I knew I was in trouble. He hit me and down I went. There was a crowd round us by this time and pride got me to my feet only to be knocked down again. The Aussies were cheering and my lot were shouting, I managed to get to my feet again and dived at him. I had him on the ground and we were rolling around on the grass, I was holding on to him for dear life, I jabbed my thumb into his eye and I knew he was hurt but by this time I was holding him round the neck whilst he began to make a strange noise and the next thing, we were being pulled apart. He beat me easily but you wouldn't have thought so, as his eye was in a mess and his face was bleeding from all the scratches. I had a cut over my eye and a thick lip.

One of the Aussies told me that I had managed to hold my own with the boxing champion of New South Wales and I knew that time I had had a lucky escape. You would have thought that I would have learnt a lesson from that but no, it was business as usual. The Aussies stopped using our NAAFI after that but we never knew if they did so through choice or if they had been ordered to.

It was no easy life being in the jungle but I believe I was at my best there, a better man. I was at least able to prove to myself what I was capable of and I always took care of the new lads, showing them what to do and what I had learned from the Ghurkas. It made me think of what the major had said about me when I was on my first charge, him not knowing whether I was a follower or a leader. I had certainly led myself and the lads into a lot of trouble. I had often thought, 'If only I didn't drink,' or, 'If only I could take orders.' It was always, 'f only, if only'. If only things had been different but maybe not, that wouldn't have been me!

Life as a bad soldier was not easy. However, just some of the time it did manage to be great fun and on one of our many drinking escapades on Penang we ended up in a bar called the Craven A. It was in this bar that Charlie and I chatted up two gorgeous looking girls using our limited pidgin English of, 'You, me jig-a-jig!' After a couple of drinks and to the great envy of the other lads, we left the bar with the girls and got into a couple of trishaws. We had only travelled about a hundred yards down the road, when I heard Charlie, who was in the front trishaw, bellowing loudly to me. I had been busy snogging my girl and so hadn't quite understood what he was saying but next minute, I saw him leap out of the trishaw, pull his girl out and smack her one! I then heard him shout, 'It's a fella.' I turned round to look back at my girl but she had already taken off like a bat out of hell! I was left spitting and rubbing my mouth as they disappeared off into the distance. Charlie and I, of course, saw the funny side and as we were joined by the lads we all fell about with laughter. Needless to say we had the piss taken out of us for a long time afterwards.

During all this time I was still disobeying orders which resulted either in seven days' detention or stoppage of pay and so when Paul, Ian and I decided to take any leave that we had left and go to Penang for a holiday, I only had half of the money that they had. This, needless to say, did not deter us and it was still, 'Penang, here we come.' After three days we were skint and unable to get any more tick from the brothel Sing Tom Lom. We decided we would have to go back to camp but we didn't go back empty handed, we took Diamond Lil back with us! We moved our three beds into an empty billet and arranged for some of the lads to bring us food from the cook house.

Word soon got round the camp that Lil was with us and within a couple of days about five more of the lads joined us and hey, it was party time. We charged five dollars a shag and for the rest of our leave we never ran short of money. Whenever Lil needed to go out of the billet to the shower blocks etc, we dressed her up in our army uniforms and one of us would escort her, to make sure she didn't give herself away with her broken English or with her constant nattering. When our ten days' leave ended we managed to smuggle Lil out of the camp and return her to Penang. Diamond Lil, what a woman! How we managed to get away with it all beats me, perhaps those in charge thought, 'Anything to keep the troops happy!'

After that happy holiday we were sent back into the jungle for the last time, to work at a place called Grik, a town close to the border with Thailand. Once again, we were road building through deep jungle. It was tough but we were told that we had done a good job and made good progress. It was here that I got bull leeches on my balls, sick with dysentery and where a tick buried itself in my head! Other than that, life was good. It was here also where we had a tiger visit us. It used to come to the edge of camp, looking for scraps in the waste pit. The first time I heard it growl it frightened me to death: it sounded as if it was just next to me when in fact it was about a hundred yards away. No one ever saw the actual tiger, just its huge paw marks that it left in the mud.

We had practically finished building the road when a message came through for us to pack up and return to headquarters at Butterworth. Back at camp, the full squadron was put on standby, all leave was cancelled and no-one was to phone home or even to write a letter home. We knew that something big was happening but we would never have guessed what. Three days later we were told that the French were in retreat from what was then known as French Indochina. The British and the Americans were deciding just what to do! Would it be the British into Laos or the Americans into Vietnam? What a decision to have to make. Manoeuvres started after that and Captain Clarke, who was in charge of our troop, suggested that I go on the sick because he didn't want anything to go wrong! I thought he was OK, he was a decent bloke who had worked his way up through the ranks and so I did as he asked and went on the sick. There were only about twenty of us left in camp and so everywhere seemed strangely quiet. However, I still managed to get myself into trouble. I could hardly believe it! So, I was on the sick and this corporal, who I didn't know very well, came into the billet where I was sleeping. He told me to go on parade and I told him I was on the sick. He then told me that he was giving me a direct order to go on parade. Sure enough it was a power in the wrong hands scenario and so I told him to go fuck himself and to stop annoying me. Next thing there was a sergeant with the corporal and I was on another charge of disobeying orders. It was no big deal; goodness knows how many of that same charge I'd had!

The most senior soldier left in the camp was a staff sergeant and I was marched into his office where I had to stand in front of him and wait to be reprimanded for my latest antics. He sat there looking very relaxed and just stared at me whilst the corporal read out the charge. All the while I was trying hard not to smile. When the corporal had finished the staff sergeant looked at me for a few seconds more, took off his glasses then very deliberately he tapped them on his desk and said, "This is a very serious offence." Well, I just burst out laughing and the more he told me to control myself the more uncontrollable my laughter became, until I had tears running down my face. He told the sergeant to take me outside in order to compose myself, a thing that I was finding incredibly hard to do. However, the sergeant was trying his best with me, saying, "Look, let's just get this over with, please." He then turned to the corporal and said that he would see him later! I steadied myself and so back into the office we went but as soon as I saw the glasses again I just burst out laughing, laughing so much I had bellyache. Somehow though, I did manage to accept my punishment of fourteen days' stoppage of pay. The corporal left me in bed the next day.

Eventually the manoeuvres finished, everyone returned to camp and life got back to normal, except that I was becoming more and more uncontrollable, to the point where the junior N.C.Os. more or less stopped giving me orders and the more senior officers, when they saw me, seemed to look the other way. Then one day out of the blue Captain Clarke came to see me to tell me I was to do a nine mile bash with him! The pair of us were taken out to the middle of nowhere with our backpacks, water and weapons and just left there. He turned to me and said, "Right, Lettice, I keep hearing all these stories

about you, so let's see just how tough you really are."
My first thought was that I was to get a good hiding,
which I had no doubt he could have done, so I just
gritted my teeth, shrugged my shoulders and prepared
myself. He seemed to understand what I was thinking
and he just smiled to himself and shook his head gently,
saying that he didn't mean in that way. He then just
picked up his gear, told me to do the same and when we
were ready he said, "OK then, let's see what you are
made of." We set off running and for a fair distance I
was able to keep pace with him. The heat and humidity
were unbearable but I was determined not to be beaten
by him. When he took a drink of water I took a drink of
water: when he glanced at me I glanced at him. No
quarter was given. We had gone about seven miles
before I started to spew up and to become somewhat
delirious. I rested for just a couple of minutes then
started running again. A couple of minutes later I was on
the floor and spewing again. I looked towards Captain
Clarke through my bleary eyes, but he just told me to
stand up and to be a man, to finish what we had started,

that there was less than two miles to go and that I could do it.

It was then that I realized he wasn't just trying to break me or to pummel me into the ground. I stood up and started running again and then, with about a mile to go, he took the pack off my back and carried it for me. He was determined that I would finish. With roughly three hundred yards to camp we stopped, he poured what little water he had left over my head, told me he knew I would do it, gave me my backpack and off we went again. There was a look of surprise on quite a few faces as, a few minutes later, we ran back into camp. Captain Clarke had beaten me hands down but he didn't want to humiliate me. He was quite a man! I wonder now if it had all been just a little too late for it to have changed my attitude and my life in the army.

Not much after the run I was back to my old self and going AWOL! I had gone to Penang with a few of the lads and had decided that I would stay on rather than go back to camp. Three days later I was spotted by the military police but I didn't go quietly and during the tussle, my thumb was broken. I was still given fourteen days in the guard room. When I was released, and in order to recover from my broken thumb, I was again sent to the retreat in the Cameron Highlands. It was OK, but very quiet and no trouble, but I was still getting drunk. When I got back to Butterworth it was just the same as before, drink and trouble. I would go into the corporals' mess just to cause trouble, when really I was just putting on a show for my mates.

I was in the NAAFI one time when somebody came in to tell me I was on guard duty. I didn't believe him at first but he convinced me to go and look at the notice board. Sure enough, my name was there. All my mates were at the back of me taking the piss because of course, the last time I did guard duty was when I lost my rifle! I just thought, 'What twats.' I went to the armoury and after a bit of an argument I signed for a Sten gun: these, though, were usually only issued to officers. There I was, with three other lads, stood outside the guard room. They all looked dead smart and then there was me! I just looked a mess and having come straight from drinking, was there in body and that was it! The officer in charge came in to inspect us and when he saw me I thought I saw him look up to the heavens. The officers are supposed to check the guards and their weapons before they can go on duty, to ensure all present and correct. The guns are cocked and the soldier then places his nail between the breach whilst the officer looks down the barrel to see if it is clean, he then moves on to the next one. This procedure was duly carried out and I was told the Sten was filthy and to get it cleaned. After the weapons had been inspected we had to close the bolt and squeeze the trigger, which I then did. I got the shock of my life when I discharged a bullet which hit a flagpole at the back of the officer. All hell broke loose and the officer grabbed my weapon, only to then recognize it as his own gun.

Of all the weapons in the armoury, I had borrowed his and he had left it with a bullet up the spout. Who's a naughty little officer then? The armourer was in trouble, the officer was in trouble: and me? Well, they shouldn't have put me on guard duty. Somehow it all got swept under the carpet!

On the odd occasion that I would ask myself, "What would happen to me if I was in Civvie Street?" The answer would always be, 'Prison, most likely.' It also, occasionally, crossed my mind that maybe I shouldn't drink as much, but then I would dismiss that thought as quickly as it had arrived. It was about this time that I was to go into military prison, Kinrara, for the last time. The Duke of Kent was to visit our squadron. A great deal of fuss was going on and I was told to behave myself. Unfortunately, though, my mate Kinch had been locked up the night before and was in the guard room, which was a great excuse for me and for trouble! A long table had been set out under the stars and junior rank N.C.Os., dressed in white tunics, were serving the officers. At the head of the table sat the Duke and next to him was the C.O. As the evening went on the banter got louder and all looked to be having a good time, all looked to be going well. Things were about to change!

I was, of course, a little drunk and I began to think it would be a good laugh to sneak up behind the Duke, grab him in a headlock and demand that my mate Kinch be released from the guard room. The lads were laughing and egging me on and the next thing, I was down on my belly, crawling towards him. Suddenly there was an officer standing in front of me saying, "Whatever it is you are up to, you can forget it." I stood up, mission abandoned and I went back to the NAAFI where the lads were laughing and calling me a barmy bastard. That night was to prove just how barmy I was, as I had decided to break Kinch out of the guard room myself. As it happened, three or four of the lads also thought it was a good idea and joined me in the great break out. All hell broke loose again, but this time it ended with the guards being ordered to load their weapons and point them at us! The guard commander, who I had never seen before, was bang out of order when he thumped the smallest of us lads in the face. I went for him but was immediately held back by both N.C.Os. and officers. It was mayhem, total chaos and the poor guards with the weapons had no idea what to do. Captain Clarke stepped in, took charge and the five of us were lined up in front of him at which point I said, "Bollocks to you lot, I refuse to soldier." I then stripped naked and walked into the cell next to Kinch, who called me a nut case and then roared with laughter. At my court martial, and before they passed sentence, they read out a list of all my offences, from past to present. I could not believe it. I had thirty-two offences of disobeying direct orders, twenty-three of which had been within the last twelve months. It didn't sound good but, as I had been in the guard room six weeks awaiting my court martial, I was only sentenced to fifty-six days.

The time I spent awaiting my court martial wasn't that bad really. Every day the guard would take me for a shower and I would sit in the NAAFI with just a towel wrapped around me. Whilst there I would have about three pints of Tiger beer with the lads, laughing and joking with them about my sentence and them telling me that the firing squad were out there practising every day. It would then be, "See you tomorrow, lads," and I would be taken back to my cell. It was all quite civilised. The corporal who was on duty on 'break out' night was back on guard duty and I couldn't wait to see him. Nothing, however could have prepared me for what he said to me. He told me that he had heard stories about Lettice but that he hadn't realised that I was Lettice. He then showed me a photo of his wife, saying that when I got out of 'nick' I should go and stay with them for the weekend and that it might help to put things right! There was no mistaking what he meant and my mind went back to the episode with Ellie. What a tosser!. I told him to fuck off and to stay out of my way.

The corporal in charge of the Regimental Police was called Corporal Gale and needless to say, we called him Windy. He made life easy for me and for that I liked him. He allowed me to wear shorts and flip flops but, so that things wouldn't reflect badly on him, I agreed that on the day of my court martial I would wear my uniform. After I had been sentenced Windy was my escort to Kinrara. We were handcuffed together and taken to the railway station where we were to get the overnight train to Kuala Lumpur. As we got on the train Windy took the handcuffs off. He also took away my bootlaces. We went to the bar and had a drink and we were like two buddies, sat there chatting over our beers. Windy put the handcuffs back on as we arrived in Kuala Lumpur early the next morning. An army truck was waiting to take us on to Kinrara, where I of course knew what lay before me but Windy had no idea what to expect. I warned him to leave me to it and not to try to help but he thought he knew better. He was kept in there with me for an hour and had to march at double pace as I was put through the same old rigmarole. The camp commander was new to me: he was a major in the Horse Guards. When I was marched before him he already had my documents in front of him and was busy reading them, then without even looking up he said, "You are wasting mine and the staff's time, march him out." I knew I was in for a rough time. Still, it was only for fifty six days, I could do that standing on my head. By the next morning I was ready for inspection. I had swapped all my crap gear with someone who had got out that morning and was wearing something half decent. When the commandant got to my bed, I don't think he was overjoyed when he saw everything was immaculate and even though I knew the ropes, I still made a fatal mistake of turning my head as my bed was tipped over. I doubled up as the pacing stick sank into my guts. "Stand still," screamed the staff sergeant. So it had started. Fifty-five days to go.

The bed tipping only lasted a few days and then I was given all the shit jobs like cleaning the grease pit outside the cookhouse, where I stood waist high in greasy, smelly, slimy water, scraping the sides of the pit clean. At least I could go and shower but then I was told to do it all again, bastards. What the staff didn't know but what I knew from past experience was, that if I left a tube of toothpaste, a bar of soap – or anything, really – under the bins by the cookhouse, the Chinese man who emptied the bins would take the item and leave cigarettes there instead. Every cloud has a silver lining! Inside Kinrara we were rationed to just two cigarettes a day, one in the morning and one at night and so some of the lads thought I was an OK bloke when I was willing to share these extra cigarettes with them. I think the staff must have been told to try to break me, but I could handle anything that they dished out. There was one staff who tried harder than the others. He was a nasty piece of work and his name was Davies. I told him before I left I might meet up with him again someday!

On my release I was sitting in the back of the truck looking at Kinrara and thinking, that's it. I wasn't going to be seeing that place any more, when all of a sudden I was gripped by a sudden feeling that I was going to die. It was weird. I was very relieved when we safely made it to the railway station. A driver met me as I got off the train and he gave me the news that I had got my ticket. I was going home. The next troop ship for Blighty was to leave in ten weeks' time and for those ten weeks it seemed that I was just left to do what I wanted.

It slowly dawned on me that I would very soon be returning to reality and that I needed to sort myself out. I could not continue to behave as I had been doing whilst in the army. I had been in Malaya for two and a half years and although I had little experience with girls when I arrived, I'd had real sex with an older woman, met numerous prostitutes, and had several memorable working trips into the jungle: had seen a rhino, a python, lots of snakes and had been in close proximity to a tiger. I had seen the enemy close up and had been in a military prison three times. I was only twenty-one and my military career was coming to an end, but not quite yet. I said goodbye to my pals and boarded the train which took two days to get to Singapore. It was there that I boarded H.M.S *Nevasa*, the same ship that had brought me out to the Far East just a short while ago. I had with me just a sea kit bag with a couple of shirts, some shorts, a towel, a toothbrush and some shaving gear. I was wearing flip flops. I had given the rest of my gear away as I wasn't going to be carrying it all back to Blighty. Mick Molloy had very generously given me two hundred dollars so that I would be OK to get back home.

I decided to stay off the drink until I got back, the reason being I wanted to look OK when my Dad saw me. I hadn't written home for at least two years. I was ashamed of that and also quietly ashamed that I had been kicked out of the army, although I wouldn't have admitted that to anyone at the time. I managed to stay sober for about four weeks, which was the time it took to get to Cyprus. I remember going ashore at Limassol, going into a bar run by a German woman and meeting up with some lads who were stationed there and the rest of the night I can only recall in flashes. I remember being chased by some military police down the quayside towards a small naval boat that was sat in the water, about six feet below us. The navy lads on board were shouting at me to jump down, which I did. I remember speeding out to a troop ship, pulling up beside it and somehow I must have managed to clamber up the steps that ran up the side of the ship to the deck, because it was there where I remember facing a sea of naval officers. The next morning a sergeant major from the Royal Engineers came to see me, to tell me that they had been considering what to do with me and had decided to put me ashore at Gibraltar for a court martial. I sort of raised my eyes at this but he then went on to say that he had been looking through my records and he had seen that I had already been discharged and that he didn't see what good it would do to charge me again! What he was prepared to do was to try to square things with the ship's captain if I promised to stay off the drink for the rest of the trip home. I promised. I thanked him and he said he would come to see me later. I spent the rest of the day deep in thought, coming to the conclusion that every time I went on the booze I got into trouble but it still didn't cross my mind that I may have a problem. The Sergeant Major returned telling me he had managed to sort it but that I would have to apologise to the ship's captain. By the time I tracked the captain down he was sat with a group of his officers and they were having a meal. The waiter who was serving his table saw me and asked me what I wanted. When I told him he said, "Don't be daft," but I insisted and so he went over to the captain and whispered into his ear. The captain looked round, as did all his officers. He walked slowly towards me, stopping directly in front of me. He was an imposing figure of a man and he towered above me. "Well?" he said. I tried my best to explain that I had stayed off the drink all the way from Singapore until the day we docked in Cyprus and that I had only intended to have a couple of drinks and that I didn't know what trouble had happened because I could not remember. I apologised and said that I wouldn't drink for the rest of the voyage. He listened intently, accepted my apology then turned to return to his table but after a couple of strides he turned to face me again saying, "By the way, I am not a big fat arsed bastard, it's just that I wear tight shorts!" He then returned to his table, where he must have told the tale to his officers as there was a sudden burst of loud laughter and that was it!

It was September 1961 and what a wonderful sight and a great feeling it was to be sailing towards the white cliffs and the lush green fields of England. When we docked at

Southampton the sergeant major who had helped me in Cyprus was on hand to help me again, providing me with a shirt, trousers and a jacket. There were roughly two and a half thousand troops on that ship and I was the first to disembark. Customs were on the dockside and they asked me where my gear was. I replied, "This is it." The next question was, had I anything to declare. "No," I answered. Then, "How long have you been in the Far East?" "Two and a half years," and I emptied my bag on the table and all I had was a razor, a toothbrush, soap, a towel, and a pair of shorts.

Again the sergeant major came forward, to speak to the Customs officer. They then let me go and I just nodded to him in thanks. Everyone in the queue behind me was in uniform and carrying huge kit bags, many with extra boxes and parcels. Talk about odd man out. I stood out like a sore thumb.

There were just five of us going to Chatham and one of them asked me where my gear was. I told him I had either thrown it or given it away as I hadn't wanted to be lumbered with it all the way from Malaya. He said, "Blimey, mate, you're going to be in for it," but I just laughed, saying, "They can't do anything else to me, pal." A corporal met me at Chatham and took me to the Quarter Master's store to hand everything back that I had initially been issued with. He went through the whole list starting with boots. The reply was, "None, sir," as it was for the full list. When he had gone through the whole procedure he looked at me and said, "You won't be going anywhere, lad, you owe the army a fortune." I made no reply, just shrugged my shoulders. Sure enough, two regimental police came for me and escorted me to the commanding officer. The sergeant major was with him and I was told to wait outside while they both studied my papers. I was called back in where they handed me a one-way travel pass to Blackpool and my army discharge book which said, 'This man is being discharged for consistent breaches of discipline, retention undesirable in the interest of this service.' I was then escorted to the barrack gates and that was that! My brilliant military career really was at an end.

I truly believed that things would be different back in Civvie Street but I was wrong. I only lasted a few weeks back at home before I was asked to leave. My dad couldn't believe I was the same person that had left to go into the army. Once again it was drink and trouble. Some of my pals had got married, or were courting: one had moved to Canada. It was just Moz and me that were left out of the gang.

Rock 'n' roll wasn't the same! Jerry Lee Lewis was unable to get any new records out. Elvis had been spoiled, by Col. Tom Parker. He just seemed to make films and I didn't like the songs much. Buddy Holly had been killed in a plane crash, Little Richard had turned to religion and The Platters were not making any new records. There was only Fats Domino left. Elvis made a comeback eventually. He was different but he was great. I had been in the army for three years and seventy-four days and although I had got the order of the boot, I enjoyed the time I was in. For someone who had never been anywhere, the army allowed me to see places I only read about. Gibralter, the Suez Canal, the Red Sea, Aden: across the Indian Ocean to Ceylon (Sri Lanka) Singapore, Malaya and Borneo. Not bad for a pie-eater (a Wiganer) – quite a journey. Six weeks to sail to Singapore.

In 1962, I met a beautiful girl from Glasgow: my Jaci. A few months later in April 1963, we were married and within two years I was the proud father of a boy (John) and a girl (Kerry). Later we had another girl, (Debbie). I had everything that a man could wish for. Uunfortunately, I continued to drink.

Drink always prevented me from being the husband and father I wanted to be and my journey through alcoholism was chaotic, destructive and painful. You can only say sorry so many times! I hated myself for what I'd become. Things I disliked about other people, I was now doing myself. But most of all I kept hurting people I love. I eventually reached the lowest point of my life and asked for help. I have not had a drink since (one day at a time). I was now able to accept that I was an alcoholic. Slowly things got better and I have now been sober for 37 years. I love the life I have today. I am so fortunate I am still married to my beautiful Jaci, 53 years – amazing!

I was about to start a new life that would lead me to 'Jimbopo'. I was born James, then I was little Jimmy, then Jim. Eventually my friends called me Jimbo. It stayed that way until I started writing poetry, late in life. My first poem was a long time on the production line.

Five years ago, I got cancer. I had the tumour removed, followed by intensive treatments and am now doing well. The recovery period was long and hard but it gave me the time to seriously reflect on my life. I then turned my hand to writing poetry. My poetry is life in rhyme. I write it as it is and enjoy speaking at various venues. I find it very rewarding sharing my poetry. Life has been good to me!

POEMS

John Barleycorn the Thief

A love was born, John Barleycorn
the moment that we met
In sharing joy and boisterous times
you aided and abet.

You poured yourself all over me
such merry making days.
Consumed by you, what could I do
united in our ways.

Good times rolled on, John Barleycorn
lots of fun and laughter.

Not a care in the world
just one more drink
no consequence after.

More of yourself you gave to me
a true and trusted friend.

Depending on you, through and through
I prayed it would never end.

Then out of the blue, a terrible thought!

Conscience, I believe it's called.

I shouldn't keep hurting people I love
at which I'm most appalled.

Feeling uneasy yet soldiering on
my burden gets quite a load.So, another wee goldie,
another wee dram

and another one just for the road

Changing times, John Barleycorn
the future for us looks bleak.

You've slowly turned
your back on me
we hardly ever speak.

Your moods are such a worry
I fear you've gained control.

My spirits breaking, piece by piece
my body and my soul.

Then came the time, John Barleycorn
a time of pain and sorrow.

Support from you had fallen through
so I'll give you up "Tomorrow"

No! now is the time it must be done
of this I must endeavour
I can no longer hide, I'm dying inside.

The good times are gone forever.

You came and stole my mind from me
John Barleycorn the thief.

Freebooter you became to take
giving nought but grief.

At last I know just who you are
a tempter I clearly see

So I'll fight you tooth and nail, old friend
And what will be will be.

With battle lines drawn, John Barleycorn
'tis a time that I shall relish.

With your golden glow
we trade blow for blow
to thee I intend to banish.

I charge you to settle
let conflict cease
Consign ourselves to finding peace.

Combat is over, a truce agreed
to leave you alone, is all that we need.

There's no turning back, John Barleycorn
agreement has been made.

1 live a good life, a day at a time
while you lurk in the shade.

I know you keep your eye on me
hoping that I'll fall
But today I'm the man I want to be
I no longer hear your call.

Strange to look back
at the life I once led
and look where I am today
in sharing ourselves, the way we did
there was always a price to pay.
Respect has grown from deep inside
now that I do without.

You're the master of me, John Barleycorn
of that I have no doubt.

Listen

I'm told I must leave,
that you want my land.
That cannot be right
I don't understand.

So I want you to listen
to what I have to say.

I'm not here on this Earth
just to obey.

This land was my father's
and his father's before.

You have so much
and still you want more.
I'm shown no respect
dismissed as a fool.

I'm loving my country
but not those who rule.

Shouting out loud
I demand to be heard.
You thought I would leave
and not say a word.
People join in
who believe in my plight.

Starting to protest
and willing to fight.

Police with batons
try to make us retreat
but we're staying put
we will not be beat.
More people uprising
who have slept in the past,
now wanting change.

A future to last

You've known for some time
this day would arrive.

You drink the fine wine,
while we just survive.

Is this what it takes
to get your attention?

You send in the troops
with an act of aggression.

But we'll stand our ground
What else can we do?
This land I behold
is so good, for so few.

I begged you to listen
you didn't take heed.
Conflicts now started
it's need against greed.

Barricade your doors

we're going to break in.
You've now started something
that you cannot win.

Your last chance to listen
is now far too late.
Time's on our side
to determine your fate.

Rebellion. Rebellion
is our call to arms.

But to kill our own people,
gives cause for alarm.
Abhorring my neighbour
who once was a friend.

I know how it started
But how will it end?

It's now civil war
the fightings intense,
the killing of children
just doesn't make sense.
Mindless bloodshed.

Not what I intended.
When you told me to leave
I only defended

in the quiet of night
I afford a few tears
no way did I think
we'd be fighting for years.
I hear of bad things

that go on every day
with war comes the horror
the price we all pay.

With hideous contempt
there's murder and rape
of mothers and wives
who have no escape.
Take turns to abuse
a son or a daughter
screaming with terror
like lambs to the slaughter

Barbaric and savage
it's tribe against tribe
horrors take place
too hard to describe.
Our land is destroyed
smashed up into pieces
with no running water
brings the spread of diseases.

No food in our bellies
no water to drink.

No bullets to fire
now close to the brink.

A truce is declared
and with it some hope.
The long tug – of – war
has run out of rope.

I look all around me

in total dismay.

Fine buildings are ruins,
our land a dull grey.
What have we done
to our once splendid land?
You told me to leave
and it got out of hand.

If only you'd listened,
it's you we all blame.

But we must all share
The burden of shame.
Guilt and remorse
I feel empty inside.

For all that remains
is a great, huge divide.

Different cultures
of different faiths.

With different intentions
and different aims.

Who can we trust?
we look at each other
are you a spy?
or are you a brother?

A new dawn rises
and with it the sun.

A struggle for power
has already begun.

Discussions take place,
that's the only solution
to talk and to listen
with great resolution.
With honest intent
there's a chance to succeed
to treat men all equal
of colour and creed.

"Listen"

Website

A silver cobweb sways
reflects in the sun
The spider is patient
awaiting his lunch
Silence is broken
by the chirping of birds
scratching the earth
searching for worms
A blackbird defending
what he's claimed his patch
His mate's on the nest
the eggs soon to hatch
A ladybird resting
as though it's the king
but nothing compares
to the butterfly's wing
Kissing the blossom
a hard working bee
creating the fruit
on an old apple tree
Swifts oh so graceful
nearly touching the ground

collecting the insects
hardly making a sound.

A hawk up above
hovers and waits
the pigeon below
unaware of his fate
Scavengers watching
crows and magpies
when all had their fill
it's left to the flies
Twilight arrives
and out come the bats
A frenzy of feeding
on midges and gnats
The mice in the field
are out on the prowl
But waiting to swoop
the sharp eared owl
In the darkness of night
come the slugs and the frogs
snails in their shells
no match for hedgehogs
The cobwebs still there
the following day
and wrapped in a parcel
the spider's prey.

Who am I to *judge*

It's said that all men are equal
and I feel I must agree.

For a blind man, might see his life
that much clearer than me.
Some men are strong,
some men are weak.

Some men are killers whilst others are meek. Some men
are hated and some men adored.

Some men are rich
while others are poor.Yet The weak man
could be a killer.

The strong man
the one that's meek.

The hated man,
could be a honest man.

The adored man
just a sneak.

The poor man
may have nothing,
yet contented with his life.
The rich man could live

a stressful life
and be dead at 35.

I dedicate this next poem to my grandmother, who taught me right from wrong. She was my inspiration and mentor in life.

Grandma Phoebe Jane

I went to Wigan
when I were four
To live in me Grandma's house.
Two uncles were there
Harry and Joe.

Joe were quiet as a mouse
Harry were little
but by heck he were tough
Them coal miners were all the same.

And he'd walk five miles
to work down pit
then five miles home again.

An old tin bath, in front of fire
was how we all kept clean
Thi scrubbed me up fit to admire
an' dried to a rosy red gleam.

Me gran looked at me
an shook her head
and said wi' a tear in her eye
I'm goner make sure
that tha' gets well fed
An Ah'l start wi' a right good pie.

Just look at thi' lad
she said to me,

Tha's as skinny as a rake, bout teeth.
I'll build thi' up like Superman,

I'll give thee loads of beef.

I allus felt safe in me Grandma's house.
I knew she were glad
I was there.

An' she'd pick me up
an' give me a hug,
as she sat on her
old rocking chair.

I loved her steak 'n' cowheel pie,
I were told it'd stick to me ribs.

Her pea 'n'ham broth
cooked on the bone
An I liked two penn'orth of chips,

Pigs' trotters an tripe.

Lots of scouse.

I were proper looked after me
I got good grub
in me grandma's house.

She raised me. Fit as a flea.

I pulled a face
as castor oil come out

It were horrid, an' hard to swallow
Just hold thi' nose an open thi' mouth,
malt would allus follow.

Cod liver oil I got every day,
goose grease were rubbed on me chest.
She combed me hair
an' pinched me cheeks
Then on wi' a wynciette vest.

All houses in lane
were much the same,

They just had a latch on door,
an' they had a peg-rug
in front of fire.

It warmed up flagstone floor,
a black leaded range
brushed to a shine.

Gas mantle gave us light.

A candle were lit rest of time.

To go to bed at night.

The Liptrots, next door
were Albert an Flo
wi' two lassies, Elsie 'n' Rose.
One lass wer bonny,

I liked her a lot
but t'other had a right runny nose.

Albert were a man
who liked his beer
He'd get drunk on a Friday night.
Flo meanwhile would sit by the fire,
Already prepared for the fight.

The house after that
were old Zachry an' Pat
"Gaskell" I think they were called.
They were no spring chickens
I'll tell thi' that.

Maybe a hundred years old.

When Zach passed away
an' laid out to rest.

The dressed him
in collar an' tie.

I called at house
to pay me respects
An' were grateful
for pennies on his eyes.

Bobby Ramsbottom,
were a right dour man.

I was so wrong
to think him a boor.

Beryl his wife
were allus sad,
son Freddie were
killed in the war.

All folks rallied round
to do what they could
to help them
cope wi' the pain.

But Bobby were lost,
a shell of a man.

Their lives were never the same.

Wilfred an' Fanny
were well known in lane,
Wilfred were ever so small.
Fanny were big
wi' a lovely smile,

She must have been six feet feet tall
Fanny wer funny
I've got to say, to me
she were a right good laugh
Me eyes popped out
As walked in one way
She were just
getting out of the bath.

I were froze to the spot.

In a state of shock
Big Fanny were gawping at me.
It were a moment in time
I had a mental block
I simply couldn't speak.

"Oh it's you, Jimmy lad
thank goodness for that,"

She said wi' a bit of a grin.

Go in pantry and get thee a bun,
They're in the big red tin

When winter crept in
An' frost starts to bite,
it were allus perishing cold.
An' to go to lav
outside in the yard
Thee had to be brave an bold.

" Wigan Observer "
an' " News of the World "
torn up an hung on string.

Un' to wipe thi' backside
wi' paper that hard
u'd allus make me cringe.

Upstairs were I slept
at bottom of bed.

Between feet of Harry an' Joe.

If a foot came close
to me face in night
I'd just give a bite on a toe.

Knocker up come tappin'
on window in dark,
to get thee out of bed
It were off to work wi' billy can.
"Snap" were cheese, or jam and bread.

One day I were walking

home from school
an' I found a big bone in street.

I threw it at lampost
but missed by a mile,
it were time to test me feet,
for it smashed the window
of our parish priest,
who saw me running like mad.

I let me gran down
when priest come round,
it all finished rather sad.

I wouldn't admit it, I told lie after lie.
I knew I were a total disgrace.

What hurt most of all
I clearly recall, was the look
on me grandma's face.

I fell out wi' church
not long after that,

I couldn't go to confession.

I owned up to me gran
who knew all along
It taught me a valuable lesson.

Me grandma gave me
all she could give.

The values I have today.

An' when she were ready

to leave this world,

I honest an' truly prayed.

I prayed I could die
before me gran,
my heart was in such pain.
But you don't always get
what you pray for in life.

I was taught, by my grandma
Phoebe Jane.

Gravedigger Godfrey

Gravedigger Godfrey
was preparing a grave.
For a man that was known
as Big Bad Dave.

He smiled to himself
as he measured the plot,
for Dave was now heading
to a place very hot.

Godfrey with spade
fairly warmed to the task.

Rolled up his sleeves,
a quick nip from his flask.
You had to admire
the plan of his toil,
allowing one drink
for each foot of soil.

The vicar on passing
with slight hesitation.
Glanced down in the hole,
with great reservation.

Make sure it's dug deep
just in case.

I'm told that he died,
with a smirk on his face.

Godfrey kept digging
for all he was worth.
Lost three pints of sweat,
two inch from his girth.
He stopped for a rest
at nine feet deep.
Completely exhausted,
he fell fast asleep.

The vicar was tasting,
the fruit from the vine.
Well known for investing
in fine altar wine.

He starts to rehearse
for his sermon next day,
strolled through the graveyard,
commencing to pray.

"We are gathered here"
was all vicar said.
Waking up Godfrey,

My God, am I dead?

He broke the world record,

with one mighty leap.

The vicar took off,
he's now herding sheep.

Maurice Hare was a larger than life man and the youngest of four friends, who met up as often as possible to wage war on the golf course.

Maurice used the word " awesome" quite often when he hit a good shot. We shared lots of banter, good old fashioned fun. On occasion, Maurice would ask Rodney, who had been in the merchant navy as a young man, "Rodney, tell us a story of when you were sailing the South China Seas."

The men are getting restless, ah arr. 'Twas a dark and stormy night. We would burst out laughing like kids, but no story was ever told.

Sadly Maurice got melanoma cancer and had to have two of his toes removed to save his life, it didn't work. I miss him to this day. I decided to write the story that was never told.

Awesome *Maurice*

In the South China Sea
A long time ago.

Storm clouds gathered
wind starts to blow.

An old sailing ship
two days from its port
laden with cargo
it's going to export.
Upsurging of waves
make the crew ill at ease.

Bad stories were told
of the South China Seas
The captain is steadfast
no cause for alarm
he sends for the bosun
who's told to stay calm.

No stars could be seen
on that dark stormy night
the ship tossed about
a most fearsome sight.
Two men on the deck
were washed overboard.
While other men prayed
please save us Lord.

Battling on through
the black watery grave
the captain's one thought
the men he must save.
Strapped to the wheel
he grimly holds tight
setting his mind
to get through the night.
Ever so slightly
the storm seemed to ease.
Suddenly stopping
and then perfect peace.
Men so exhausted
can't believe they'd survived
thanking the captain
who's barely alive.
Carried by stretcher
down to his bunk
convincing him slowly
the ship hadn't sunk.

Bosun stood proudly
counting the crew
Praising them all
for what they'd come through,
men stood in awe
as the captain improved.
Who sends for the bosun
its now time we moved.
Sets course to find land
amid all the cheers.

"Well done, lads" says bosun
to quell any fears.

From the crows-nest
a shout, "Land ahoy"
Euphoria erupts
a great feeling of joy.

Men were in tears
having won the fight.

And praise be to heaven
on that dark stormy night.

Tales are still told
of the South China Seas.
Of pirates and shipwrecks
and of awesome Maurice.
Who survived for a while
against terrible foes.
They knew him thereafter
as Maurice Three-toes.
.His bosun, named Odd-knee
had stories to tell
of Davy Jones' locker
a deep wishing well.

His one wish for Maurice
calm peaceful rest.

As Davy Jones' locker
Protects our treasure chest.

Miss Attitude

I think what I'll do
when I leave school
is probably be a pop star.

I'll become very rich
acting the bitch
I've had plenty of practice so far.
I could be a model
and become quite wealthy,

I pose all the time
when taking a selfie.

What about politics,
how hard can that be?

To tell a few lies
and appear on TV.

It just crossed my mind
I could be a preacher,
just work on a Sunday,
or perhaps be a teacher!

Woodland Bark

A woodland bark
awaits resurrection.
Buds on the trees
a spring intervention.
Snowdrops and crocus
blend with each other.
Bluebells and daffodils
a carpet of cover.

High in the trees
crows come alive.
Squabble and squawk
as to who will survive.
The shriek of a jackdaw
expressing a scowl.

Watching all this
a small tawny owl.

Wood pigeon and doves
Coo-cooing combine.

A song thrush duets
the sound so divine.

A cuckoo calls out
for a nest she can borrow.

Laying one egg
in the home of a sparrow.

Houston Calling

Houston calling
World within grasp.
Heavenly body,
Mysterious mask.

Houston calling.
Limousine car.
Bodyguards, beauty,
Iconic star.

Houston calling.
Powder the nose.
Petals cascade,
wilting black rose.

Houston calling.
Need to confide.
Poppy is serving,
the serpent inside.
Houston calling.

No time to rejoice.
Fragile the image,
destroyed is the voice.

Houston calling.
Touchdown in view.
Memoir of passing.
"I will always love you"

Mind Games

A shiver on the spine
a candle blows out.
Humming so softly
bursting to shout.

The breathing uneasy
a heave of the chest
all of a sudden
strange things manifest.

Demons abound
in dark creepy places.
A gathering of swine
saliva on faces
spewing out evil.

A deep growling bark
red eyes of satan
burn in the dark.
Shaking with terror
becoming much colder.

Lucifer's presence
is here on my shoulder.

Choking on brimstone
that sulphurous smell.
Is this the end?

At the gates of hell.
Praise be to God
my soul He redeemed
in saving my mind
all's not what it seemed.

Blushing

Shy is the maiden
asked for a dance.
Fingertips touch
love at first glance,
look deep in the eyes
of blushing young miss,
raising hand slowly
to give tender kiss.
Shy is the maiden
asked for a dance,
is it seduction?
or the start of romance?

Watching

A young boy sits
on a rock among rubble.

He shouldn't be there
it's asking for trouble.

A teardrop falls
he's feeling so lonely.
Watching some boys,
thinking if only.

Just a few days ago
they all played together.
Having a laugh,
doing whatever.

Now he's an outcast,
they call him a traitor.

He decides he must go,
will try again later.

His mother's upset,
her son's heart is in pain
His father stays strong
as he tries to explain,
that he works for who governs,
has sworn his allegiance.

That it would be treason,
to show disobedience.

He comforts his son
stroking his hair,
tells him the truth
all that he dare.

Talks to the boy
with a slow calming voice.

Leaving his son
to make his own choice.

The young boy listened
as to what father said,
causing him turmoil,
a pain in his head.
Tossing and turning
most of the night.

But eager to rise.
As dark turns to light

Same rock, same time
the following day.
Different games
were now being played.
No longer a ball,
no longer had fun.

All carried sticks
and pretend it's a gun.

A young boy sits

on a rock among rubble.
He's about to explode
in bursting the bubble.
The mob came over,
they tell him to go.
Now he stands up,
to strike the first blow.

He takes a good beating
but he's severed the ties.
No more heartache,
he no longer cries.

It no longer matters,
who's wrong, who's right.

They may be just kids
But have chosen to fight.

As time passed by
the boys disappear,
forced from their homes,
living in fear.

In need of protection,
hungry and cold,
one has been killed,
is what he's been told.

A young boy sits
on a rock among rubble,
alone with his thoughts
of this terrible trouble.

He looks all around

at wide empty spaces,
the absence of noise
and of missing faces.

During my sober years I have often told of the time I was so drunk, that I had killed some chickens. 1 woke up with lots of blood, muck, feathers and chickens, scattered over the bedroom. I was shocked, as I couldn't remember doing it!

As years passed by, one chap when he saw me about to talk would comment, "Here we go again, chickens." He was only kidding but 1 decided to make light of it and introduce him to some chickens.

The Morning After

Give it a rest dear
you don't have to shout.

My head is like jelly
wobbling about.

I feel that I'm dying!

I just want to sleep.
Having nice dreams
of Little Bo Peep.

You don't have to swear dear!
use language like that.

I can prove that I'm a willey
that I'm not a twat.

Bang goes the door
gone is the nag.
open the window
and light up a fag.

I throw back the shoulders
and stand up like a man.
Bracing myself
to face my least fan,

The silence is deafening

I sway to and fro.

With hands on her hips
she's ready to blow.

You are disgusting!
you always get drunk.

The smell is revolting
you stink like a skunk.
Don't laugh! It's not funny
have you no shame?

To say it's the others
that you're not to blame.

So! Who was you with?
Clive Little, Rob Dickens.

At the back of my mind
something about chickens!

I start to recall
where we had been.

I sang karaoke
to *Dancing Queen*.

Clive was a riot
they thought him a star.
Well he wouldn't know
of that nice gay bar.
Fighting them off
they thought him a flirt.

1 later explained
of his bright pink shirt.

Rob was in stitches
watching the chase.

He fell to his knees
a total disgrace.
Laughing so much
caused pain in his tummy.
Shouting out loud
I want my mummy.

Then what happened
is a bit of a mess.

For I woke up this morning
wearing a dress.

It must be a nightmare
I used straw for a wig.
Chasing some cows
and grunt like a pig.

How did you get home?
a taxi of course.

Then what's that in the garden?
I'm sure it's a horse.

I believe you've gone mad
you drive me insane.
How come it's got feathers
tied in its mane?

Ding chickens!